Laban M. T Hill, James Edward Bates

The Story of Damon and Pythias

Laban M. T Hill, James Edward Bates

The Story of Damon and Pythias

ISBN/EAN: 9783743317536

Manufactured in Europe, USA, Canada, Australia, Japa

Cover: Foto ©ninafisch / pixelio.de

Manufactured and distributed by brebook publishing software (www.brebook.com)

Laban M. T Hill, James Edward Bates

The Story of Damon and Pythias

THE STORY

OF

DAMON AND PYTHIAS.

"BEHOLD HOW GOOD AND HOW PLEASANT IT IS
FOR BRETHREN TO DWELL TOGETHER IN UNITY."

BOSTON:
ALFRED MUDGE & SON, PRINTERS,
34 SCHOOL STREET.
1878.

COPYRIGHT,
BY LABAN M. T. HILL,
1878.

TO THE MEMBERS

OF THE

ORDER OF THE KNIGHTS OF PYTHIAS

This Poem is Dedicated

IN TESTIMONY OF THE FRATERNAL REGARD OF

THE AUTHOR.

THE STORY OF DAMON AND PYTHIAS.

CANTO I.

ARGUMENT.

PALÆMON, the Pythagorean, pursuing his homeward voyage, sails by night along the coast of Sicily, and in the morning arrives at his destination. — Palæmon in Syracuse. — He relates how the Syracusans defeated the great expedition sent against them by the Athenians. — Necropolis. — The siege and fall of Acragas described. — Alarm of the Sicilians. — The popular assembly is convened at Syracuse. — The speech of Dionysius; its effect on the common people. — They take the lives of their military commanders, and then imprudently put Dionysius among the Board of Generals.

The scene of each Canto is in Sicily. The narrative proceeds in the assumed authorship of Palæmon, who is represented as being a member of the secret Brotherhood to which Damon and Pythias belonged and an eye-witness of the events described.

I.

THE shades of evening fall upon the deep,
On yonder fading headland, and the strand,
Fast mingling with its fringe of springing surf,
As onward rolls the dusky car of Night.

O'er all comes darkness save the lofty mount
Beyond Catana,[1] that 'mid pitchy cloud
And glowing ashes lifts its gloomy flames,
Licking the vaulted sky with sullen roar
Which louder than the moaning surge is heard.

Like Pythia's fire this Pharos ever burns,[2]
A beacon to the wary mariner.

The breath of Boreas fills the swelling sail
As to the south our creaking prow is turned;
And 'mid the silent watches of the night,
We plough with swifter course the watery waste,
While to our destined port we nearer draw.
Above, Orion, sheathed in gold,[3] pursues
His way, the glittering sword upon his thigh,
Upon his mightful arm, the lion's hide;
The weeping Hyades,[4] in endless grief

---

[1] Ætna: see Appendix A.

[2] The priestess of the celebrated oracle of the Pythian Apollo at Delphi was called The Pythia. On the Pythian altar, placed before the statue of the god in the most sacred recess of the temple, burnt an eternal fire.

[3] "Armatumque auro circumspicit Oriona." — *Virgil: Æn.*, III, 517.

[4] *Hyades.* The seven stars in the head of the Bull. The story is that the daughters of Atlas, King of Mauritania, were so afflicted by the loss of their brother, Hyas, who had been killed in the chase, that they died of grief. They were five or seven in number. After their death they were changed into the constellation. The setting of the Hyades at both morning and even-

And radiant beauty, mourn a brother's fate;
Brightly on Evening's brow fair Hesperus gleams;
The Dioscuri,[1] saving from the storm
The voyager upon Poseidon's realm;
The greater Arctus, guide of Grecian keels,
The lesser, by Phœnician helmsmen sought;[2]
Selené's silver disk, full-orbed and clear,

---

ing twilight was to the Greeks and Romans a sure sign of rainy weather, these two periods falling respectively in April and November. To this the derivation of the word — from ὕειν, to *rain* — refers. Demoustier thus neatly tells the fable: —

" . . . . Les Hyades pleurent leur frère
Qu'un monstre dévorant ravit à leur amour.
Le roi des cieux, touché de leur douleur amère
En vain les transporta dans son brillant séjour."
Lettres à Emilie.

[1] *Dioscuri.* A collective surname of Castor and Pollux, the tutelary gods of hospitality and navigation. In astronomy, the constellation of the Gemini. Among other appellations these deities had acquired that of "sailor-helpers," ἀρωγοναύται. Poseidon (Neptune) had given them, as the reward of their brotherly love, command over the winds and waves. They appeared after storms at the extremities of the masts and yards of ships, — a phenomenon nowadays called "the fire of St. Elmo." St. Ermo, however, seems to have been the older Italian name. See the once famous dithyramb, Bacco in Toscana, of Redi, in which he describes the constellation as

" L'oricrinite stelle di *Santermo.*"

[2] According to Ovid, the Greek navigator steered by the greater, the Phœnician by the lesser, Bear: —

" Esse duas Arctos; quarum Cynosura petatur
Sidoniis, Helicen Graia carina notet."

In tremulous vista, mirrored on the flood;
And countless clusterings of dazzling ray, —
Await the lingering dawn and cheer our path.

Purpling the sombre bourn of sea and sky,
The first faint glow of rosy morning springs.
Night's splendors pass away, the heavens pale,
And Amphitrité's[1] breast no more is gemmed
With gold, reflected from the canopy
Above. In chariot drawn by tireless steeds,
Eos, all-welcome Goddess of the Dawn,
Chases the wavering shadows to their grave
And clothes the orient slope with saffron hue,
Until, emerging from the watery verge,
The God of Day begins his upward course.
North, east, and south the mounds of ocean gleam,
Stretching away beyond the range of sight;
But westward, on Trinacria's[2] shore, appears
The golden shield[3] that marks our journey's end.

---

[1] Amphitrité was the wife of Poseidon, and so, by metonymy, the *sea*.

[2] Trinacria was an epithet of Sicily, and referred, of course, to the three principal promontories of the island (τρεῖς, ἄκραι).

[3] In that quarter of Syracuse called Ortygia stood a lofty temple dedicated to Athena, on the top of which was a shield, visible from afar at sea.

Sailors on the point of leaving the port were accustomed to take from an altar in the temple of the Olympian Hera a cup containing certain offerings; these they threw into the sea when they lost sight of the landmark on the temple of Athena.

II.

Belovéd Syracuse![1] again thy walls
Enclose the weary wanderer from afar,
Who, homeward turning, seeks his native land.
Again, with eager steps, I press the soil
That bare me, and, with tearful eyes, would fain
Behold the friends of youth now passed away.
Some 'mid the winds and waves have read their doom ;
Others, beneath war's hurtling tempest fell,
Careless of life if for their country spent ;
Or, bowed with years, in peaceful rest were laid.
How does my heart, O Philadelphus, mourn
For those who nevermore may know its faith !

Again I view the towering citadel
That frowns above Ortygia's sea-worn bounds ;
The massive ramparts whose high battlements
Protect our firesides from the invading foe ;
The statues, groves, and altars of the gods ;
The stately temple of Olympian Zeus,
And many scenes, forgotten, but recalled
As with attentive gaze I onward move.
"Not all things unto all men should be told " ;[2]
But unto thee, my friend, I freely show
Such pleasure and such grief as may betide.

---

[1] See Appendix B.
[2] One of the prudential maxims of the Pythagoreans.

III.

Around me stand memorials of the days,
When, like a torrent from the mountain-side,
The strangers from beyond the ocean bore
The whetted steel, — Enyo, Ares,[1] both
Approving, — and with spear and iron sleet,
The mighty, climbing billow of their host
Sought to o'erthrow our city from its base.
When from Athenæ their armada sailed [2]
To compass and to waste our fatherland,
The loud-tongued trumpet sounded, and 't is said
The herald's voice invoked the gods in prayer, —
As if high heaven could smile on impious deeds!
Then was the pæan chanted, while the chiefs
Libations made, in gold and silver cups.
Their passage to Corcyra straight they took,
And at Corcyra joining their allies,
A thousand vessels bore them on their way, —
Transports and triremes huge that vexed the flood,

---

[1] *Enyo, Ares.* The former, answering to the Roman Bellona, was the Greek Goddess of War; the latter —

" Gore-tainted, homicide, town-batt'rer Mars " —

seems to have been the god not only of war, but also of general slaughter and destruction.

[2] The Athenian expedition against Syracuse, to which further reference is hereafter made in the third canto of this poem, sailed from the Piræeus, the harbor of Athens, about midsummer, B. C. 415.

And groaned beneath the enginery of death ;
A swimming host of dreadful citadels,
Such as the ocean never saw before.[1]
They passed Italia's shore, and on the land,
'Neath waving plumes stirred by the breath of War,
And on the dark-blue wave, with brazen beaks,
Closed round our sacred temples and our homes,
As in the hateful bonds of servitude
They sought to lead a race in freedom born.
From yonder heights, outreaching to the main
On either side, circumvallations sprang.
Within the ever-narrowing folds begirt
The brave defenders seemed a hope forlorn,
While, life in hand, they met death's gloomy hour
As men who for their country gladly die.
Each in the common weal beheld his own,
And stood unmoved against the thickening storm.

Suns flamed and set, and seasons came and passed,
As, in unequal strife, we faced the foe,
And many a soul, 'mid deeds of deathless fame,
Went to the unseen, all-receiving shore.
Still round our crumbling ramparts, far and near,
Forests of horrent steel uprising marked
The hostile ranks whose number none might count ;

---

[1] " Ein schwimmend Heer furchtbarer Citadellen,
   (Der Ocean sah ihresgleichen nie.) "
         Schiller : Die unüberwindliche Flotte.

And the broad field of ocean to its rim
Was whitened with their sails.
                              Thus like our fount
Of Arethusa,[1] ever famed in song,
With flow unfailing and with waters clear,
Girdled with billows on yon rocky marge,
Were we environed by the clouds of war.
At last the God our earnest prayer fulfilled,
And late, but surely, sent us welcome aid.
Gylippus came, a man well versed in rules
Of strategy, an army in himself,
And with him foreign help, both ships and troops.

Thus was our city saved; for with new hope
We quickly sought the triremes and the camp
Of our beleag'rers. They, in boastful pride
Of numbers, little recked the sudden danger;
For then and afterwards, by land and sea,
The spoils, the crown of victory, were ours.
Then might you see the brave Demosthenes,
Who from Athenæ sailed to their relief,
And Nicias, great only in reverse, —
The ill-assorted leaders of our foes, —
Urge on their followers to heroic deeds.

We who were late besieged, now, in our turn,
Became besiegers, and our cause so pressed

---

[1] *Arethusa.* See description of Syracuse in Appendix B.

That soon the hostile multitudes were made
The abject prey of slavery to the spear.

Such grand events, the spoils of history,
Took place, as you and other Brothers know,
Whilst I, an exile from my native home,
Repined in loneliness on foreign shores.

IV.

I passed from crowded life and stood amid
The stillness of Necropolis, where rest,
No more disturbed by War's loud clarion,
Such as untimely, yet with glory, fell
Upon the battle-field for Fatherland.
The simple mounds of earth and heaps of stones,
Columns and tablets, and the sumptuous wealth
Of *heroa*,[1] and deep, sepulchral vaults,
Were, all alike, ingarlanded with flowers,
The yearly offering of sorrowing friends.
Near by, with teeming life and happy homes,
I saw the queenly city that they saved;
Beyond, the harbors and the dark-blue sea
O'er which the hostile armament advanced.
Around me, moving in the cooling breeze
That inland soughed, with ocean's fragrance fraught,

---

[1] *Heroa*. These were mausolea, sometimes small temples, dedicated to *heroes*.

The sad, funereal cypress waved its boughs;
The olive, with its pale-green foliage,
And Median trees, weighed down with golden fruit,
Joined in a lowly threnody, and seemed,
If such have song, to mourn the fallen brave.
As when the sleepless Eviad looks forth
And in the moonlight, from her mountain height,
Beholds Thrace white with snow, and Rhodope
Thronged with its troops of Mænad votaries,
And, lost in speechless wonder, is inspired;[1]
So, in this sacred Presence, whilst I gazed
Upon their place of life and strife and rest,
I felt my spirit moved by Power unknown,
And seemed to hear a voice divine that said, —

Here is entombed the sacred dust of those
Who, in fulfilment of their country's call,
Took life in hand and, that the State might live,
Sought death and gained an immortality.

Weep not for them! For these memorial stones
But speak the glory of the land that bore

---

[1] "Non secus in jugis
 Exsomnis stupet Euias
Hebrum prospiciens et nive candidam
 Thracen ac pede barbaro
Lustratam Rhodopen, ut mihi devio
 Ripas et vacuum nemus
Mirari libet."
           Horace: Od. III, XXV, 8.

Such heroes. A republic saved, not they,
Requires thy tears, — surviving through such loss.

The orb of nations evermore shall be
Their monument, wherever Freedom lifts
Her awful brow, and love of country fills
With holy flame the breast of humankind.

Weep not for them! They sleep in soft repose,
In blest assurance of an endless fame;
Admire their deeds, envy their glorious death,
And, like them, in thy country's need, fail not!

V.

Stranger than tongue can tell! Oh, utter woe!
But yester-eve hundreds of thousands thronged
A mighty city; and the ramparts, towers,
And massive fortresses were thickly manned
With brave defenders; and the air was filled
With mingled sounds of proud, of martial life,
Of chariot crowding chariot, of the voice,
Loud and imperious, of command, the blare
Of brazen trumpets, clash of arms, and tramp
Of faithful squadrons. From without there came
The hoarse remurmuring of besieging hosts,
Vainly advancing to the desperate charge,
And the earth-shaking impact, as the walls
Withstood the shock of hostile batteries.

Now, as the gray of early twilight yields
To morning-red, how changed is all the scene!
Throughout the vast-expanded maze of streets
No living form appears; and desolate
Seems every home; and, as amid the waste
Of barren desert, awful silence reigns.
Why do the sentinels no longer hold
Their stations on the threatened battlements?
Why are the bulwarks reft of their defence,
And e'en the citadel upon the hill?
Why is nought heard within the steadfast gates,
Save the faint murmur of the foemen's camp,
As springing daylight wakes them to their task?

The catapults, *balistæ*,[1] and huge frames
Of battering-engines that are ranged without,
Loom up like spectres through the misty air
To call on those within, now, now to haste

---

[1] The *balistæ* — the Roman military term — were adapted to project heavy stones against battlements; while the catapult discharged darts and other light missiles.

The extreme range attained by the *balista* was about a quarter of a mile. The more powerful machines of this sort could throw stones weighing three hundred-weight.

The use of such engines seems to have been very ancient. We read of Uzziah (or Azariah), King of Judah (B. C. 810), that "he made in Jerusalem engines invented by cunning men, to be on the towers and on the bulwarks, to shoot arrows and great stones withal." — 2 Chronicles xxvi, 15.

And save the city from impending fate.
In vain! It seems a city of the dead.

But look! What giant form surmounts the wall?
What bold besieger in relief against
The brightening sky? His face is swart and burned
By Lybian suns. His glittering vestments show
Barbaric splendor as of Afric's clime.
He gazes on the scene of loneliness
And, quickly turning, shouts in unknown tongue
To those without. Up climb two savage Gauls;
And then, with warlike cry and lifted spear,
Iberians, Lusitanians, Cantabri,
Campanians, dusky Lybians, and the hordes
Of every region and of every race,
Swarm through the open portals and invade
The silent ways, and, as the lightning rush
Of torrent bursting from some alpine cliff,
O'erthrow before them all that can oppose,
And with swift desolation waste the town.

The gathered wealth of nations is their spoil.
Unawed by sacred things, with step profane,
They violate the temples of the gods.
The image of divinity within
Confronts them as they enter; but alas!
The steel, stern-hearted, thirsting for its prey,
Pollutes the holy places with the blood

Of helpless thousands hid in refuge vain.
They spare nor age nor sex; but everywhere
Are plunder, rapine, and the cries of death,
With mutilated bodies of the slain.
Such was the fall of Acragas;[1] and thus
The Carthaginian army, that beneath
The ensigns of Himilco, — Hannibal
Its other chief, — three hundred thousand strong,
Crossed o'er from Lybia in certain hope
Of making conquest of Trinacria,
Sees half its work accomplished.
        Far away,
Slow moving on the weary road which leads
To Gela, throngs with slow and painful step
A countless host that in the midnight hour
Left the doomed city, and, in fearful flight,
Abandoned all in hope of saving life.
On, on they move, that population vast
Of wretched exiles, not the strong alone,
But gentle dames who sigh at thought of toil,
With tender nurselings cursed by Até's breath;
The halt, the wounded, and those bowed with age
Or sickness. Common woe unites the mass;
The helper and the holpen are as one.
The fair morn spreading on the mountain-tops
Is unto them as evening's gathering gloom.

---

[1] See Appendix C.

DAMON AND PYTHIAS. 19

When will they e'er again behold their homes?
In what far region will the lot be cast?
What Power invoked, attend their wayfaring?
Onward, for miles and miles, the unnumbered throng
Extends, funereal as the gloomy shades
Descending to the hateful Stygian flood;
While here and there, half seen through the dense
    cloud
Of swirling dust, appears the gleam of arms.
Close in the rear, to cover the long line
From the pursuit of a victorious foe,
Thousands of hoplites[1] march in serried ranks.

Now there were portion of a numerous force
That Syracusæ early sent to help
Her sister city; guessing well that should
So rich a prize fall to the invader's spoil,
Her own fair homes would next become his aim.

Returning to my native land, I saw
The mustering of this army of relief,
And, led by love of country, joined its ranks;
Then, honored with the post of chiliarch,[2]
Took part in all the fortunes of the war;
So did I witness much whereof I write.

---

[1] *Hoplites.* These were heavy-armed foot-soldiers, who fought with a long spear and a large shield, ὅπλον, whence the name.
[2] The chiliarch commanded about a thousand (1,024) men.

And why did the great city fall? By art
And nature she had seemed so doubly strong
That to assail her walls were hopeless task ;
Her sons were numberless as are the sands
Upon the shore ; e'en as the ruddy stream
Of Tagus or Pactolus [1] was their wealth ;
And as their wealth, so their magnificence.
Truly Empedocles,[2] our Brother, said,
"They built as if they were to live for aye ;
They lived as though to-morrow were life's end."
She had most timely warning. Both by land
And sea she gathered strength to meet the shock ;
Her granaries were filled ; her troops were brave
And many. With her, from the first assault,
Had been good fortune by the help of God :
The enemy's fierce onset was repulsed ;
Then the besieged, outsallying from the ports,
Drove back the foe and fired the battering-train ;

---

[1] The Pactolus was a river of Lydia, whose waters were believed to flow with golden sands. The Tagus, Po, Hebrus and Ganges had the same repute.

[2] Empedocles was a Pythagorean philosopher of Acragas, born about B. C. 450. Distinguished also as a physician and poet. After the capture of Acragas by the Carthaginians he went to the Peloponnesus and there died. The Agrigentines appear to have deserved the full force of his *bon mot*. According to Diodorus, their luxury was such that in the height of the Carthaginian siege a public decree was made that no one on guard at night should have more than one bed, one tent, one woollen blanket, and two pillows.

And when the Carthaginians broke down
The sepulchres in which reposed the dead,
And sought to use in structure of their works
The marble of the lofty monument
Wherein the body of King Theron slept,
A thunderbolt from heaven rent the tomb![1]
Forthwith religious terror filled the camp,
The shades of those disturbed appeared by night;
And then a fatal pestilence destroyed
Thousands on thousands of their wicked host.
Now, too, were seen afar in crimson ranks
Our army of relief from Syracuse,[2]
Driving before them the barbarian hordes.
Amid resounding shouts of "Χαίρετε,"[3]
We pressed within the gates and joined our friends.

Thus far all things were faring well. But now,
Alas! the sun of our prosperity,
Before so bright, moved in its downward course.
The valor of our troops and the allies,

---

[1] Such is the not improbable statement of Diodorus. Afterwards Himilco forbade the further demolition of the sepulchres, and according to the custom of his country, sacrificed a boy to Cronus (Saturn), and cast into the sea a number of human victims as offerings to Poseidon.

[2] This army, with reinforcements from Gela and Camarina, consisted of 30,000 infantry and 5,000 cavalry. A fleet of fifty galleys proceeded along the coast to co-operate with the land forces.

[3] Greek, — "Welcome."

So often tried on many a hard-fought field,
Was worthy of no cause less high than this;
The cause itself, of champions not less true.
But what availed our cause, and what availed
Its gallant votaries, while treachery
And traitorous strategy, that futile made
Our strength, prevailed, and stern necessity,
That mocks the plans of man, through instruments
Venal and base, yet powerful to command,
Had willed our fall?
                  Until the latest hour,
Amid disasters that in baleful train
Quick followed one another, and the strange
Inaction of our generals, we hoped
For victory. Our hope, alas! was vain.
But why recount the story of our fall?
How, at our coming, every chief, save one,
Of Acragas, convict of having sought
To palter with the enemy, was swept
Away, his just reward to claim in death; [1]

---

[1] The principal charge against the Agrigentine generals was that they had refused to attack the Carthagenian fugitives at the time of the victorious Syracusan advance.

According to Diodorus, the Agrigentines having met in assembly immediately after the arrival of the Syracusans, were addressed by one Menes, a Camarinæan officer, who arraigned the commanders of Acragas with violence, so exasperating the people that the accused could not be heard in their own behalf. Four of them were at once stoned to death by the enraged multitude; the fifth, Argeius, was spared on account of his youth.

How all the leaders Syracusæ sent,
Among whom was Daphnæus, were believed
To be corrupted with barbaric gold
And secretly our overthrow to plot;
How futile were the means whereby they feigned
To battle with the bold invader's ranks;
How much by conflicts ill-advised they lost,
And how by inactivity, much more;
How by the hostile squadron prize was made
Of vessels bringing food for our relief,
And famine drove us from the fated walls.

Let other lips than mine the tale repeat
Of those dark days; the memory alone
Were sad enough to patriotic heart
Without relation, though events more sad
And still more hurtful to the public weal
Were nigh at hand. Onward the unnumbered throng
Slow moves o'er lofty mountain and the waste
Of sultry plain. No rest and no delay
For the outwanderers, as with feebler step,
Weary and wayworn, smitten by the breath
Of the sirocco,—laden with the heat
O'er the broad ocean borne from sun-trod realms
Of Afric deserts,—and by thirst consumed,
And famine, Gela's sheltering walls they seek,
And Syracuse.

VI.

Ah! what a panic fear
Was spreading now throughout Trinacria!
What multitudes were surging through our gates
Haply to find a refuge from the storm
Without! How many even left our shores
And in Italia secure remained
Until the tempest should be overpast!
What indignation justly filled the breast
Of every Syracusan when he heard
The dark recital of calamity
And learned the conduct of the faithless chiefs!
How quickly uprose all, and, grasping sword
And spear, with dauntless hearts prepared to meet
Amain the merciless and savage foe!

But what to do? And who should lead us forth?
On this seemed hinging our republic's fate.
And so the crier proclamation made
That the whole body of our citizens
Should meet together in *ecclesia*,[1]
And, duly hearing, in their sovereign power
Whate'er the public good required decree.

---

[1] The *ecclesia* was a general assembly of the citizens, in which they met in their sovereign power to debate and determine upon such matters of public interest as might come before them These assemblies were either *ordinary* or *extraordinary*. The present *ecclesia* was specially convened.

VII.

A silence as of darkest midnight stilled
The vast assembly; for the destiny
Of thousands upon thousands seemed to rest
Upon some word unspoken; while the past,
The present, and the future of the State
Were waiting for the moment when the voice
Of some true patriot, gifted with the power
Of knowledge and the power of eloquence,
Should be uplifted, and with trumpet-sound
Proclaim, whether for weal or woe, the truth.
For here were met the wisest and the best
Of Syracusæ, — veterans well versed
And tried in dark and complicate affairs,
The sages who had always guided well
In times of danger. Who of these grave men
Would foremost claim respectful audience?

Long, long we waited; then, at last, we saw,
Slowly uprising, one before unknown, —
Unknown at least to me; almost unknown
To all, save two or three who greeted him,
And in acclaim hailed Dionysius.[1]
"But stop! Shall he, a youth, a stripling, speak
Before his elders? He, a beggar scribe,
Fresh from the public office, counsel those

---

[1] See Appendix D.

Who roll in wealth and power imperial?"
Listen! He mounts the *bema*,[1] and, with eye
That flashes like the noonday bright, begins: —

"Syracusans! If learning, wealth, age, rank,
Or glorious service in the commonwealth,
Or Eloquence divine, with golden mouth,
Could add unto the words of him who speaks
The simple truth, and faithfully proclaims
Our perils and the duties of the hour,
I, with becoming modesty, would sit
In silence. But the knowledge of our ills,
And of their guilty causes, is not far
To seek. Nor were it difficult to tell
What patriotic duty bids us do;
Nor matters it by whom, or in what words,
So that in drastic shape the truth appear.

"Menaced by self-same dangers, all alike,
Whether in council or on battle-field,
Must labor for our threatened fatherland,
Unmindful of false titles that too oft,
Amid the easy, sluggish flow of peace,
Have marred our democratic polity.
Then I, among the youngest and the least
Of those here gathered, Dionysius,

---

[1] The *bema* was a raised platform from which the speakers addressed the assembly.

Son of Hermocrates and citizen
Of Syracusæ, and, as such, your peer,
May claim with deference the right to speak,
Both for myself and for the common folk,
Such things as long ago should have been said.

" Still lives our commonwealth, illustrious
In honor, dignity, and in the fame
Of her ancestral freedom; but alas!
Her life seems bounded by the speeding hour,
Except your instant foresight, wisdom, will,
Swiftly transferred to action, shall avail.
The bloody ensigns of the cruel foe,
From victory to victory advanced,
And coming ever nearer to our gates,
Are raised above the great metropolis
Of Acragas, which next to Syracuse
Was the most famous in Trinacria.
Selinus, Himera, and Acragas,
Each in its turn, have fallen! We almost
Alone survive the ruin of our land.
Against our walls, our homes, and sacred fanes,
Will now advance the grim barbarian hordes,
Unsparing, merciless, of humankind
The offscouring, the refuse, and reproach.
Those horrid scenes of ruin, rapine, death,
Of sacrilege and crimes too great to name,
Which, making desolate our sister-towns,

Seem as the memory of some hideous dream,
Having no counterpart in real things,
May soon, too soon, be witnessed by ourselves.
Act instantly, O men of Syracuse!
From such dread fate our common country save!
With noble purpose, living to be free,
Our lives to yield before our liberties,
Let us go forth to meet the hostile wave
Already curving to its thunderous fall!

" But lo! there sit the authors of our ills!
Within this solemn gathering I behold
The very men who caused these fearful woes!
The very chiefs, with sinful gold corrupt,
Who come with blood-stained hands from Acragas,
And dare obtrude themselves within this presence!
There are the dark-souled traitors whose misdeeds
Call now for retribution swift and sure!

" They enter here and tarry with the brand
Of wicked, heinous crime upon their brows.
The death of those, our fellow-citizens,
Who fell as victims of this treachery;
The utter desolation of the host
Which, hopeless of relief, has left the homes
Of Acragas to crowd within our gates;
This terror and despair; the storm of war
That beats upon our walls; this urgent need

Of meeting in assembly to avert
The greatest danger in our history, —
For all this let them answer with their lives!
For treason less than this the citizens
Of Acragas in fury stoned to death
Their own commanders. Then shall these escape
The fearful doom that justly waits a traitor?
Ay! now and here, O men of Syracuse,
Fulfil the call of our outragéd State!
For long delays of law wait not, wait not
For process and slow hearing, but forthwith,
No more respecting legal forms, proceed
To execute our vengeance and destroy
These foul betrayers of the country's cause!
Seize them, and kill them! Let them not escape!"

As, when the storm-clouds hurry o'er the main.
The pleasant, sheening day is swept away;
And dark sea-waves are whitened by the blast
And lifted to the skies, and hurricanes
Whelm in the roaring surge the laboring bark
That erst in steady course was voyaging on,
So as the words to vengeance urging fell
Upon our common people, always quick
The swiftest means to grasp, albeit rude,
To right the public wrongs, and here alert
And eager that some one among themselves
Should boldly utter what their hearts desired,

They rose with outcries, and in haste of hate
Assailed the guilty generals, and strove
To take their lives. The Archons and all such
As ranked among the Great Ones of the State,—
Save two or three, the friends of him who spake,—
The kinsmen and the opulent compeers
Of the accused, opposing force to force,
Yet with unequal strength, resistance made.
Threatenings of vengeance, shouts of death were
    heard;
Contending throngs commingled in a strife
That, 'mid the rage of swelling conflict, armed
The maddened hand of brother against brother,
The son against the son of Syracuse.
What frenzy, in our nation's history
Before unknown! What wild delirium
Of passion! Solemn augury of days
That were too soon to come! As messenger
Divinely sent to mark the end of life
And shadow forth the crossing of the stream
Whose sluggish flow may never be repassed,
This woe unspeakable arose, the hope
And promise of our State to scoff and mock.

At last the tumult and contention ceased,
Reason held sway; but of the generals,—
So sudden was their doom,— but two remained;
The others, eight in number, quickly made

Full expiation of all crimes, in death,
Even as Dionysius had required.

Forthwith the Archons who presided, bound
By oath of office to maintain the laws,
To punish the infraction then and there,
As best they could, amid the general strife,
Declared of Dionysius the offence
As a disturber of the public peace;
And in consideration of his crime
Imposed on him a penalty to pay —
Because their power no further might extend —
Of seven gold talents to the public use.

Then uprose one Philistus,[1] who in wealth
Held rank among the foremost in the State,
And said: —
    "Archons and men of Syracuse!
I here produce and pay the fine imposed.

---

[1] Philistus was born at Syracuse in the year B. C. 431, and was accordingly of the same age as Dionysius. He studied at Athens under Isocrates. At first in high favor with Dionysius, he was afterwards banished by him. Having been recalled from banishment by Dionysius the Younger, he lost his life in defending him against Dion (358).

Philistus wrote a history of Syracuse, including the events of the reign of Dionysius the Elder. He also wrote a life of Dionysius the Younger. Cicero and Quintilian rank him with Thucydides, but his works are lost. This is the more unfortunate because the two Dionysii are sovereigns of whom we know little save from their enemies.

It were unjust that he who freely spake
So truthfully upon the grave offence
Of traitors, recreant to their solemn trust,
Who wafted them unto a traitor's doom
By zealous words which showed his reckless love
Of freedom and his hate of treachery,
Should so be silenced. From my ample means
Into the public treasury I pay
That which to him in poverty is denied.
Let him continue! Let him frankly tell
The dangers and the duties of the hour.
May the great gods inspire him, without fear
To give wise counsel in the times of need,
And to his thoughts a ready utterance lend!
Let him go boldly on, as he began.
This let him do, and though such penalties
Should fall upon him through the livelong day,
Till sinks the sun beyond those western hills,
I -- I engage to pay them to the State."

And then was Dionysius by these words
Urged on to speak in boldness what he would,
And in unseemly phrase, yet well adapt
To gain the sympathy and stir the souls
Of those who listened to his bitter words,
Showered as swift arrows on our many faults
Of statecraft and of public management.
He sought approval of the doom of them
That fell as victims of the people's rage,

And then, in energetic speech, alleged
The causing cause of our calamities: —

That our impending woes were but the fruit
Of false administering of our affairs
By wealthy men, and by autocrators,
Who, in subversion of true policy,
And to perpetuate long-settled power,
Forever sought the Commons to exclude
From any portion in the public charge;
And thus, while private fortunes were enlarged,
Matters of highest moment, which required
The help of all, received the aid of none;
And thus disasters overwhelmed the State.

Striving were these men for plutocracy,
Denying to the honorable poor
Official station or regard or name.
From this had sprung the source of gravest ills.

That they alone should be put in command
And fill the offices of peace and war,
Who were distinguished, not by wealth or rank,
But by devotion to the common weal.
The rich and titled, conscious of their power,
And holding all beneath them in contempt,
Would at the public cost new treasures gain,
And recklessly conduct affairs of State,
While men of little fortune, yet inspired
With patriotic purpose, — having nought

To shield them in wrong-doing, or promote
Their welfare, or make glorious their name,
Save a repute for honesty and zeal, —
Would well and faithfully perform the trust.
He sought not for preferment, but should they,
The common people, of whom he was one,
Or such as he had blamed, in time require
His aid in conduct of the State's defence,
Then or thereafter, he would welcome death
Before defeat or treason to his charge.

These reasonings, with others of such sort
As well might please the many, were set forth
By Dionysius. After him his friends
Philistus and one Hipparinus spake.

And then the populace in wild acclaim,
Thrusting aside the warnings Prudence gave,
At once raised Dionysius to the Board
Of Generals, and him, with others, put
In joint authority o'er all the troops.

Thus from the surge of desolating war,
Bursting with dreadful force upon the land,
And from the bitter strife within our gates,
And slaying of our fellow-citizens, —
As from Medusa's blood the wingéd steed,
As Aphrodité from the foaming wave,
This man, before unknown, had sprung to power.

CANTO II.

ARGUMENT.

CALLISTE, the home of Pythias, described. An interview between Pythias and Dioné, his wife, on the eve of the former's departure for Syracuse. — Dionysius artfully gains the good-will of the Syracusans, and, finally, after procuring the removal of his associates in command, is appointed generalissimo. Thereupon, having obtained formal authority to keep a body-guard, he leads the Syracusan army against the Carthaginians — The treasonable purpose of Dionysius, to make himself tyrant, discovered; sudden return of Damon, Pythias, and others to Syracuse. They exclude Dionysius, from the city. Attempt of the latter to enter by force. A midnight battle at the gate of Achradina. The assailants, having destroyed this gate by fire, occupy the town and overcome all resistance. Pythias, after conducting a most heroic defence, is wounded and thought to be slain. Damon is captured, condemned to death, and committed to the prison of Lithotomiæ. — Dionysius, Tyrant of Syracuse.

I.

FAR from our city's turmoil and its wealth
Of splendor, on the margin of a stream
Whose tranquil flow, pure, liquid silver, glides[1]

---

[1] " S'alcun giammai tra frondeggianti rive
   Puro vide stagnar liquido argento."
   Tasso: G. L., Canto XIII, LX.

Unto the shore that greets the ruddy glow
Of springing morn, to find its ocean-grave,
Stands a fair cottage, the abode of peace
And happiness. Calliste was it named.
And truly does it seem to be a home
Of beauty ; as that far-off, shining isle
By Delos crowned, amid the Ægean main.[1]
With many a tendril o'er its whited walls
Cluster the purple honors of the vine ;
And mingling with their shade, the laurel waves
Above the doorway and the rudely carved
Apollo, emblem of the radiant god.[2]
Here bloom soft hyacinths and violets pale,
The tamarisk and saffron marigold ;
And, pure and calm, beneath the chequered woof
Which glooms the streamlet's marge, the lily sleeps.
Here daffodils retain a tear for Him[3]
Whom, robed in fatal beauty, Echo sought
In hopeless love ; while murmuring wood and fount
Recall the memory of her vanished form.

The crimson glory of the scented rose
Is scattered o'er the greensward, and the gold

---

[1] The island of Calliste ("*most beautiful*"), known later as Thera.

[2] In front of a Greek house not infrequently stood some emblem of Apollo Agyieus. The laurel was sacred to him.

[3] Narcissus.

Laburnum and althea's purple hue,
And thyme to which the wandering bees oft roam
From Hybla's lofty height.[1]
                    On either side
The streamlet, from its brink, where wildly flowers
The oleander, to the distant plain
Which bears lentiscus, with its fragrant bole
O'ershadowed by the palm-tree's giant leaves,
And rocky crag where the lone cactus grows, —
A bosky canopy, forever crowned
With deathless verdure, clothes the gladsome earth
In varied charms, and makes, beneath its bowers,
A milder sunlight and a sky more blue.

And 'mid thick, arching foliage, in relief,
Glimmers the yellow of the ripening fruit, —
Fruit such as, warded by Night's daughters, erst
Shone bright in garden of Hesperides.[2]

Lo! To the westward, seen o'er yon dark glen,
The vast, majestic domes of mountains rise,

---

[1] There were three Hyblas in ancient Sicily; one (now Paterno) in the east part of the island, northwest of Catana; Hybla *minor* or Heræa, southeast of Catana, celebrated for its honey, which rivalled that of Mt. Hymettus,— to-day, Calatagirone; and Hybla *parva*, afterwards Megara, on the southeast coast near Syracuse. Hybla *minor* is here referred to.

[2] The islands of the Hesperides were placed on the western confines of the world. Here the daughters of Hesperis, three

Reaching to heaven and bordering on the stars.
When, midway, drives athwart their dizzy slope
The racking mist, their massive tops do seem
In fancy to the startled eye of him
Who gazes, always to fall, yet falling not.
There, since the world began, have ever stood
Those everlasting ramparts, reared by hand
Of Nature.
   As slow sinks the orb of day
Beyond their summits, the empurpled clouds
Long glowing, bathed in saddened light, appear
As the last smile of one beloved, who dies.[1]

And thither look, where, miles on miles away,
Yet seeming near in this pellucid air,
Looms Ætna's grisly and stupendous form.[2]

---

or seven in number, guarded the golden apples which Gæa gave to Hera on the day of her marriage with Zeus.

 Ovid represents that the leaves and branches of the garden, as well as its fruit, were of gold: —

> "Arboreæ frondes, auro radiante nitentes
> Ex auro ramos, ex auro poma ferentes."

 One of the twelve labors imposed on Hercules was to obtain these golden apples.

  [1] "Oui, dans ces jours d'automne où la nature expire
   A ses regards voilés je trouve plus d'attraits;
   C'est l'adieu d'un ami, c'est le dernier sourire
   Des lèvres que la mort va fermer pour jamais."
         Lamartine: L'Automne.

 [2] See Appendix A.

Alone it stands, and frowns o'er land and sea.
The fertile, swelling fields, which gird its base
And, fearful, clamber on its rock-bound sides,
Shrink back from bleak and thunder-rifted heights,
Crusted and iron-like, worn by fire and ice,
By wind and tempest, through the centuries.

Ever above it whirls a rolling dun
Of smoke, winnowed and storm-tossed by the gale;
Ever, 'mid darkness, plumed by spires of flame,
It towers a beacon to the coming dawn.

Now greater shadows mark the evening hour,
While yet the sun, unwilling to depart,
Lingers in cloudland and upon the hills.
The painted birds no longer charm the ear
Of him who tarries in this blest retreat,
With chant and carol blithe and liquid trill.
Only the lonely nightingale is heard.

II.

Ah! who is she that o'er the threshold comes,
And, on the pearly ashes of the day
Bereft of all its life of sunshine, looks
In thoughtful sadness toward the fading west?
Is it a tear, betraying silently
Some grief untold, that gathers 'neath her brow?

Does one so lovely mourn amid these scenes
Of beauty, whereof she, the fairest gem,
Seems as the living utterance and the soul?

Deep-crimson cheeks to which the rose is pale,
And coral lips to mock Love's burning sigh,
A wealth of waving tresses, half embraced
By fillet wrought of blue inlaced with gold,
Bright eyes, full orbed, whose dark yet lustrous
    depths
Reveal the fate of all on whom they gaze,
A youthful form, of ravishing contour,
Unfolded by Sicilia's genial skies,
Commingle in the rounded charms of her,
The matchless pride of him whose own she is.

And he, whose bride she is, now comes without
And stands beside her. In his noble form
Are gracefulness and glow of manly strength,
And martial port that fittingly beseems
The knightly hero of the battle-field.
And in his heart burns bright a quenchless flame,
Whence, full displayed in word and deed, doth spring
The never-failing tenderness wherewith
He worships her, the worshipper of him.
Here hath she found her longing soul's desire;
And to its cherished presence closer clings
Than doth the mantling ivy to the oak.

With mutual gaze, bespeaking mutual love,
Together, hand in hand, they wend their way
To rustic seat that by the streamlet's marge
Invites to pleasing rest.   And there embraced
By his fond arms, she says with tearful sigh: —

"And must to-morrow, Pythias, bring the hour
When thou wilt leave me, — homeless, save with thee?
Shall these affairs of state forever rend
The happy tissues of our household joys?
This night were an Elysium to me, —
Ay! every fleeting moment, crowned with bliss. —
Save that o'er-envious time too soon doth speed
Our parting."
    " Sad to me, Dioné, is
The rayless sunlight that looks not on thee
Beside me; hard it is to part from her
For whom my soul in absence maketh moan.
Thou, best-beloved, art the guiding star
To me of life and being.   Thy fair form
Preserves its imaged throne on battle-field,
By camp-fire, and amid the toilsome march
Through desert waste, in dreams and everywhere.
But now once more this sorrow comes.   Again,
As shrills the loud-tongued trumpet, must I hence.
But, that performed which sacred duty bids,
I'll haste to lay my laurels at thy feet.
My heart distraught by separation, yet

Unmoved by change of time or place, is thine.
And thou, Dioné, as in the happy hour
When we came one, wouldst not forsake thy choice?"

"Ah! Pythias, every bliss that home can give
Without thee is in vain, for that thou art
My all in all of every inmost joy.
For such as thou I sighed e'er I had found
Thee: but when found, that all my former life
Was passed without the fulness of thy love.
That which thou art to me, my soul knows well, —
' Faithful — as is the shepherd's watchful pride,
True — as the helm the bark's protecting guide,
Firm — as the shaft that props the towering dome,
Sweet — as to shipwrecked seamen land and home,
Lovely — as child, a parent's sole delight,
Radiant — as morn that breaks a stormy night,
Grateful — as streams, that in some deep recess
With rills unhoped the panting traveller bless,
Is he that links to mine his chain of life,
Names himself lord and deigns to call me wife.'" [1]

"Forever, fair Dioné, may high heaven
Preserve thee in its charge! For aye

---

[1] Æschylus: Agamemnon, 896–901 (Dindorf's text).
This paraphrase was originally published in England in the Quarterly Review. The name of the author is unknown. The annotator trusts that the beauty of the lines may, to some extent, tend to justify the anomaly of their insertion here.

May the firm bond of mutual love unite
Our hearts in one! No greater boon I ask,
Nor greater blessing could the God bestow.
Though hard the fate that I must from thee part,
Leaving these happy scenes for war and strife,
Yet comes the hour — such is my heartfelt prayer —
When every danger threatening to the State
Shall in the past be merged, and soon again
Our days with joy be crowned, our nights with bliss.
But while the foe is hurrying to our gates
The patriot son of Syracuse must stand
As watchful sentinel at duty's post.
To-morrow, then, a sad farewell to thee,
And to our children, sunlight of our home,
Whose prattling child-life, happy as their dreams,
Knows not the cloud that makes our pathway dark.
Remember me in absence, who shall e'er
Within my heart of hearts remember them
Without whose love that heart would cease to beat."

III.

But now, my Philadelphus, came the hour
When hapless after-wit might hope in vain
To wrestle with a peril to the State
More fearful than the murky cloud of war
Still battening o'er the spoils of Acragas.
Sad hour for Syracusan liberty!

Not to her freeborn sons upon the foe
Advancing, pointed ruthlessly and stern
Its index-finger, but on men bowed down
Beneath a tyranny whose giant strength
O'ermastered both their fortunes and their lives.

Fools! they that saw not danger ever clear;
And worse than folly! that to him who wrought
Their ruin they had rashly given that
Whereby his horrid treason was made sure.

How well do I recall the glorious day
When our new leaders in command brought forth,
With martial pomp, the flower of Syracuse!
As were reviewed the endless, glittering ranks
Filled with heroic purpose and inspired
With hope of victory, proud swelled the breasts
Of those who gazed, and all to come seemed bright.
The humble artisan, returning home,
Greeted his household with a happier smile;
The child in mimic war-play was more brave;
The veteran, bent with years, was young again
In pleasant reminiscence of the past;
The mother clasped her babe, now reassured
That freedom and not bondage was its lot.

How fair the mocking fabric! soon, too soon,
To crumble, perish, and to fade away;

As when in dreams the fainting traveller views
A waving verdure and pure living streams,
And wakes amid the boundless desert waste.

IV.

Three months have passed since that tumultuous day
When Dionysius was so quickly raised
To sit among his elders in the Board
Of Generals. But since he took command
He has, despite his boastful promises,
Done nought except to aggrandize his power,
Increase his following, and make clear the way
For that which only when too late is known.

No sooner, aided by the popular breeze
Of favor quick excited by his art,
Was he securely fixed in leadership,
Than all the exiles who aforetime sought
Under Hermocrates[1] to overthrow
Our democratic system, were recalled.
These were his old-time comrades and allies,
Ingrained with hatred of our polity.

But Dionysius making fair pretence
That they, subordinate to his control,

---

[1] Not the Hermocrates previously mentioned. Dionysius afterwards married the daughter of the one here named.

Would help to serve against the common foe,
The people let them come within the gates.
Then boldly from the outset he proclaimed,
Both in our public meetings and without,
That his associates in joint command,
Men older than himself and better tried,
Were traitors to the cause, and so refused
To meet in conference with them or lend aid
In any of their plans of strategy.
Such crimination, oft repeated, gained
An easy credit with the multitude,
Who now, in very truth, believed that he
Alone was faithful to the public trust.
On all save him they looked with scorn; on him
With pride as one that owed his rank to them,
Their spokesman and the champion of their rights,
A man most watchful of their interests,
The hope and mainstay of our liberties.
So each ensuing day made him more great,
And more bemasked his crafty purposes.
Erelong with separate command he marched
To Gela and there tarried for a while.
Near by was camped the enemy in force;
Yet not against the foe was his advance.

Two factions were there of Geloans, — one,
Of wealthy men composed; the other, ranged
In bitter opposition, of the poor.

But Dionysius took the part of those
Of no estate, and through a form of vote
Condemnatory of the richer class,
Whom he accused of treason, put to death
The sons of fortune and confiscate made
Their property. The money so acquired
He lavishly bestowed throughout his camp
And on the common people of the town.

On every side his praise was loudly told;
The glad Geloan Demos voted thanks
In commendation of his services,
And swiftly sent the vote to Syracuse
By special envoys.

     'T was a stated day
Of yearly festival in Syracuse,
When Dionysius, as if triumphing,
Returned in fitting time to meet the wild
And heartfelt greeting of the populace,
Elated by the words that Gela sent.

From out the theatre a countless throng
Was pouring down the hillside as he came.
With loud huzzas they welcomed him. They pressed
Around and eagerly besought how fared
Himilco and the Carthaginians.
To every one his answer was the same : —

"Speak not to me of foreign foes; your foes
Within, those chieftains whom with me you placed
To lead your armies, are more deadly far
Than such as muster in the open field.
To me through secret envoy was it told
By him whose ensigns soon are to advance
Against our walls, that as my price of guilt,
Would I but let my colleagues do their will,
A greater portion should be mine than theirs.
Crushed both by this and other cogent proof
That my associates would betray the State,
I scorn to stay within their fellowship.
To-morrow, at the public gathering,
To you and them I yield my public trust."

Nor idle was his threat; for on the day
Ensuing, this grave charge, with many more,
Was made by him before the citizens
For common counsel in assembly met.
Filled was the multitude with bitter rage
Against the men he charged with treachery;
But outcries of expostulation, fear,
Quick followed, when the chief they held to be
Their only refuge, faithful to his word,
Yielded to them, its givers, his command.

This might not be! With acclamations loud,
Thrusting from place the other generals,

In him alone they vested leadership,
And granted him therein full power to act.
Thereon he moved the passing of a vote
Whereby the soldiers should be doubly paid;
And this, not without gain to him, secured,
He summoned our whole military strength
To be prepared to march in his command
Leontini; for what purpose none
Could tell. Not all went forth; but those alone
Who seemed more friendly to himself. With them
He pitched his camp beneath the Leontine walls
And near the citadel. When came the noon
Of night, his trusty intimates and he,
With outcries loud and hurryings to and fro,
Excited through the ranks a false alarm;
And while the army, doubtful and confused,
Was filled with fear, he and his friends retired,
As if for safety, to the citadel.

Thence issuing at the dawn, he wide proclaimed
That enemies within the camp had sought
His life and failed by reason of his flight;
And wounds he showed in token of his words.
Those in collusion with him told the same.
Then feigning that the troops about him formed —
As only all within his levy might —
A lawfully sufficient gathering,
Together with the rabble of the town,

To act as an assembly of the State,
Of them he boldly asked, and had conferred
By formal vote, the power to keep retained
Six hundred veterans as a body-guard.
Enlisting twice the number, he delayed
No longer, but with his whole force returned
To Syracuse. There he remained secure
Behind Ortygia's massive battlements.[1]

From us who had opposed the grant of power
To him alone, now murmurings were heard
Against him. Ever growing seemed his strength
Beyond due bounds. At first a youth unknown,
He sprang at once to take the foremost rank
Within the people's gift. Aforetime poor,
He now was rich in Gela's blood-stained spoils.
He shared before with others his command;
These gone, his sway was sole and absolute.
He had marched forth as well became his rank,
But now had he returned in kingly pomp.

---

[1] Diodorus must be in error when he states that Dionysius began to rule immediately after his return from Leontini. This is obvious from the historian's subsequent statement that the Syracusan assembly, the *ecclesia*, was in full operation at this period, and that to this body Dionysius was compelled to appeal in order to get rid of Daphnæus and Demarchus, the most powerful of his adversaries. One or two other facts mentioned by Diodorus make it apparent that the tyranny was not established until after the defeat of the Syracusans at Gela.

Much had he promised, nought had he performed.
Himilco was approaching. Why did he
Who was the common people's trusted chief
Supinely wait our ruin, and avoid
To meet him on the battle-field, or there
Where Gela tottered to her fall, unless,
Not guiltless of the crime on others charged,
Vassal of hostile gold, he only strove
His country's life, as tyrant, to outlive?
Such words were uttered now not secretly,
But openly, throughout the public ways.
The dread of some disaster, dimly seen
Yet terrible, was ever in our breasts;
We knew not when or whence it was come, —
Whether from him whom we had armed with power,
Or from the swarthy foe in open field.

But suddenly throughout the walls is heard
The stirring din of warlike preparation.
For Dionysius, conscious that the hour
Supreme of his ambition must delay,
Yet fearful of inaction, gives the word,
Commanding all our forces, both by land
And sea, to put themselves in readiness
To move at once on Gela and engage
The enemy.
            Straightway by day and night
Our armorers and shipwrights ply their task.

Soon, everything prepared, a mighty host,
'Mid cheering loud and far prolonged, goes forth
In proud array and discipline complete,
The chieftain with his life-guard in the van.

And as they march, the brazen trumpet rings
Its thrilling voice across the slumbering sea;
Then from the crowded docks, in majesty,
'Mid tears, and prayers, and longings of the heart,
Seaward to Cape Pachynus, moves our fleet.

But happier they than we who here remain
To keep our vigil on the battlements.
To us is weary waiting, — unto them,
The glory and the crown of victory,
Or blissful death, if death can him befall
Who lives forever in his country's praise.
So do the sequent hours flow sadly on,
And still no tidings of the absent ones,
Until has passed that day foredoomed by fate, —
The last of Syracusan liberty.

V.

The day is ended. Gathering shadows meet,
And darkling flow o'er fading earth and sky;
And in the deep-blue offing, sunlit sails,
Which lately gleamed afar, are lost to view.

The cloud low down, that seemed a wave-worn cape,
Now vanishes, enwrapped in thickening gloom,
Whilst ocean mingles with the vault of heaven.
The lofty mountain-tops, that erst were crowned
With tinted aureoles of splendor, wrought
Of ever-changing, ever-dying light,
Soon in their desolation dimly show
Sombre and cold against the narrow west.

The day is ended. All its wondrous sheen
Of beauty and of glory is o'erpast
To regions that beyond Hesperides
Welcome the dayspring as we mourn its loss;
And Chaos' daughter, lonely Night, assumes
Her silent sceptre and her ebon throne.

How still the crowded city! From its homes, —
The regal palace and the humble cot, —
The busy marts of trade, the holy fanes
Whence mount the incensed wreaths of sacrifice,
Fewer and fainter come the sounds of life,
And voices rare are heard as in a dream.

As on the dizzy battlement I stand
Where grim Ortygia frowns along the deep,
Round me is imaged an eternal rest,
Save where the ghostly sentry walks his path,
And far below, where moans the tideless sea,

A black and tossing waste, heaving its surge
Against the massive wall and shingled strand.
What fantasy, wrought of the mournful hour,
Dwells wraith-like in my soul's inmost recess,
Giving foreboding of the presence nigh
Of whelming danger to our threatened State?
Awe is within me! For endued I seem
As one who, slumbering, in vision drear
Beholds the spectral imagery of that
Of evil which or is or is to be.
And when I see the flaming daylight dead,
It is a mystic type of mortal woes
Whose stern fulfilment is e'en now at hand, —
The laws o'erthrown, a despot put in power,
Vanished the orb of Freedom (as the sun
Of Heraclitus), nevermore to shine, —
Unless, perchance, through flow of patriot blood,
Our children may regain what we have lost.

But now slow mounts and peers athwart the flood
The gibbous moon. In ever-broadening path
Its silvery beams all-tremulous are flashed
Across the billows as they rise and fall.
Higher it sails, and, weltering no more
In ocean's verge, sheds far and wide its rays.
Again the waste of waters gleams in light,
Ploughed by the wingèd messengers of peace;
The mountain-tops stand forth like glittering snow;

And Syracusæ with her wide-spread maze
Of streets, her groves and consecrated fanes,
And massive walls, crowned with aerial towers,
Once more is seen as in the noonday bright.

Rising majestic toward the eastern marge,
Athena's temple comes again to view;
Borne to the sky above her marbled shrine,
In splendid and colossal effigy,
The goddess looks forth o'er the rolling main
And holds aloft her rounded, golden shield,
First landmark of the inbound mariner,
Last gazed upon by him that leaves our shore.

How gladsome is the scene! On distant plains
Our brethren battle for the common cause;
But here is peacefulness. The life renewed
Of whatsoe'er was beautiful before,
May well relieve the burden of my soul.

But hark! what sound is heard far, far away
Upon the road to Gela? Ever comes
A dull vibration borne upon the breeze.
Be stilled the tumult of my wildered heart!
For now, the earth, as throbbing 'neath the shock
Of numberless and onward-rushing hoofs,
Gives forth reverberations loud and clear,
To which the ocean waves in symphony
Make echoing response.

Now I discern
A dim, mysterious line, — has it no end? —
That always nearer sweeps upon its way
To Syracuse. To arms! I see the gleam
Of burnished steel on which the moonbeams flash,
And horsemen, clad in warlike panoply.
To arms! to arms! no friendly train would fly
In furious speed against our welcome walls.
Fast man the battlements in breathless haste,
And wait their coming as they swiftly spur
Their foaming steeds! Each one be at his post!
For onward, ever onward they career,
And to Ortygia now they hold their course.
They come! they come! they seek our landward
  gate,
They shout to us within; the night-guard opes
The portal! treachery? But, no! the flower,
The pride of Syracusan knights appear, —
Philetus, Pythias, Damon, Eumenes, —
Than whom the earth bears not more candid souls,
Nor more heroic on the blood-stained field, —
Dicæus, Agathon, Androsthenes,
Nicoteles, and yet three hundred more
That late went forth. They stay not, but surmount
The wall and crowd upon the battlements.
Then Pythias, first of all the surging throng
Attending, cries to me, his flaming blade
In hand, "Palæmon, wake the slumbering town

With voice to blanch the bloodless lips of death!
Secure and guard the gates! Quick, help us hold
The ramparts! For our homes, our children, wives,
And liberty, the hour of peril's nigh!
Call every manful patriot to our aid,
And bid him stand unmoved at duty's post!
'Twere now no wondrous thing that they who sleep
In yonder sacred resting-place should start
From out their graves, — should rise to our relief
And meet the coming of their traitor son."

"Treason, my Pythias?" "Ay! a treason foul,
Embodied in the person of our chief;
Our army is o'erthrown. By Gela's walls
We fought: betrayed by him, we fought in vain.
Conspiring with the enemy, he planned
Our ruin for his selfish ends. Not all
Was lost when night fell on the field; still did
We hope the morrow would bring victory.
'T was then he met his satellites; with them
He formed the purpose to return; to them,
As later known from spies who overheard,
He openly proclaimed his dark design
To make himself the lord of Syracuse.
Gela and Camarina are no more![1]

---

[1] Dionysius had abandoned both of these cities to the Carthaginians. Their inhabitants accompanied the Syracusan army in its retreat.

Our army, part corrupted by his gold,
The rest in doubt, was ordered to retreat;
And now it crowds the roads, — a woful wreck,
Slow drifting to our walls.
                              " With minds as one,
This treason to forefend, these gallant knights
Have ridden swiftly here, first messengers
Of the defeat and of the purposed crime;
And Dionysius, with his body-guard
And mercenary horde, comes close behind,
In hope to take the city by surprise.
I charge thee, O Palæmon, by the tie
Of Brotherhood that knits our hearts in one, —
And others, whom I see, — till death to stand
And shield our freedom from its traitorous foe!
All I adjure by love of Fatherland.
Let some alarm the town! let others watch
The city gates and Achradina's wall!
I hasten to the Agora. Let each
His duty find. Whether to live, or die
For cause so just upon the battle's ridge,
What matters it to patriotic souls?

" If any false there be in such an hour,
In flood of darkness may the nether world
Him overwhelm!" [1]

---

[1] The statement of Diodorus that the knights, while awaiting the arrival of Dionysius, were guilty of committing grave ex-

As when from cloudless sky,
Whilst all things sleep beneath a noontide sun,
And not a breath disturbs the pendent leaf,
Out flashes quick the riving bolt of Zeus,
And rolls the billowing thunder, peal on peal,
And man and beast affrighted, trembling stand,
Or sink to earth, — so when we hear these words
Proclaiming that the fatal hour is come,
Lost in amazement, we are reft of speech
And filled with unknown dread.

But swiftly mounts
The love of liberty to fire our hearts
With its immortal flame; and, steeled with strength
Beyond his own, springs each one to his post.
The walls are manned; the portals are made fast;

---

cesses in Ortygia, is in the highest degree improbable. They had been "prompted as it were by an instinct of divine providence"— such is the language of Diodorus — to rise against Dionysius, and had ridden swiftly to Syracuse in order to prepare to hold the city against him. That after their arrival they should have forgotten the purpose of their coming, and should have neglected to improve the brief interval allowed them for putting the town in a proper condition for its defence is incredible. It is very likely that acts of criminal violence were committed during the excitement following their return. But that the knights were responsible for such acts must seem unlikely to every intelligent reader of history. Diodorus, no doubt, took the statement in question from the narrative of Philistus, — an historian who is said in all respects to have reflected the opinions and prejudices of Dionysius.

The city through its length and breadth is roused.
Armed knights are hurrying to and fro. Throughout
The wider streets and in the market-place
Great throngs of citizens and women, pale
With fear, are met together, and await,
With sad and anxious heart, the dread event.
And yet the slow-paced moments, seeming hours,
Creep on, and Dionysius cometh not.
In peacefulness, as if in mockery,
Far toward the zenith climbs the silvery moon.
Her flood of glory overflows the land
And sparkling wave, but shows not yet his coming.
Softly the gentle land-breeze swells and dies,
Fraught with aroma of a thousand flowers;
But to our waiting, wearied hearts it bears
No whispering of the coming of his host.
Still onward goes the work of preparation.
But now the shadow of the gnomon[1] hath,
Methinks, already marked the midnight hour.
Standing on Achradina's heights, I hear
As from afar on the Geloan road
A clattering sound like that of cavalry

---

[1] The *gnomon* (γνώμων), or sun-dial, was at this period the usual instrument by means of which the ancients measured the time of day and night. It consisted of a pillar standing perpendicular in a place exposed to the sun, and by its shadow divided the day into twelve parts. The *clepsydra*, or water-clock, came into common use at a later period.

When swift it speeds along a flinty way.
Now, now, in very truth the foe draw nigh!
For from the gloom 'neath yonder beetling cliff,
With waving plume and sudden flash of steel,
Rush into view the foremost of their van,
And bold outriders shout and cheer them on.
Others succeed, and all sweep quickly forward
To Achradina's gate, and loudly cry
To open unto Dionysius. But
Their outcries are in vain; the oaken port,
Its brazen hinges guarded by stout arms
And hearts of steel, yields never to their call.
So are they well assured the truth is known,
And that by force alone they can prevail.
In desperate charge they seek to storm the wall;
And then the roar of maddening strife doth pierce
The startled ear of night.
      The clash of steel,
The high-raised voices of command; the cries
Of combatants, the groans of those who sink
Beneath the sword or from the parapet
Are headlong hurled; the cruel grief and fear
Of friends within, Death's image, ever nigh
In ever varied, ever ghastly shape,
Do weave a horror that no words can paint,
And such as may forevermore affright
The dreams of him whose eyes have seen its form.
The din of conflict louder, louder swells.

Onward dark Treason goads her craven slaves,
Bravely the sons of Freedom beat them back.
There Dionysius shines resplendently
In glittering armor; as a lioness
In Afric wilds, robbed of her tender whelps,
He rages in the thickest of the fight.
Here Pythias, chosen leader of our band,
Stands forth all-radiant in the battle-flame,
All-glorious in the justice of his cause.
Long is the contest waged, and victory
Seems ours. They yield, withdrawing from the wall,—
But only for a time. Once more the foe
The assault renew, and, prompted by their chief,
Seek, by a novel warfare, to prevail.

Near by are ready gathered from the fens
Great stores of reeds, inflammable and dry,
Such as are burned within the neighboring kilns.
Of these they bear great masses to the gate,
And build them from its base in towering pyre;
To this they put the torch. A blaze upsprings,
And, roaring skyward, quick enwraps the wall
In furious folds of fire and volumed smoke.
The patriot band, unshaken by the spear,
Is backward driven from the seething storm.
Our ranks are formed anew and take their stand
To wait the deadly onset that is nigh.
The trusty portal, charred by raging heat

DAMON AND PYTHIAS. 63

And fretted by the cankerous fires that burst
From all its surface, wastes 'neath crackling flames
Throughout; its melting fastenings bend and yield
As fiercer knocks the all-devouring fiend.

New-comers swell the hostile ranks. The night
Is near its end.
     At once, with thunder-sound,
In ruin vast, falls Achradina's gate,
And by its smothering embers grimly shows.
To those without, our small but faithful band.
We close our ranks. "Strike! strike for liberty!"
Cries Pythias; while through the yawning breach,
In countless, overpowering numbers, rush
The foe.

 · · · · · ·

    O'erwhelmed by numbers, crowded back
Into the Agora, begirt around
By levelled steel, seven knights alone resist
Of those who mustered at the midnight hour.
Now lies their chief as lifeless 'mid the slain;
Their comrades brave no more can lend them aid.
Yet still they battle, ever choosing death
Before a tyrant's chains.
      Felled to the earth
By wounds, and then a helpless captive led,
I see the closing scene in the most sad,

Terrific drama. I behold the blow
Last struck for Syracusan liberty,
And o'er the city's latest champion rise,
In blood-bought triumph, Dionysius' power.

And only these resist? Alas! 't is so.
But one by one they fall, till Damon, left
Alone, begirt by enemies, stands o'er
His country's grave.
     " Yield quickly or you die ! "
They shout. His answer is in deeds, not words :
And by his blade, swift-flashing as the light,
Two more are wafted to the shadowy realm.
But look! he sinks! Ah! no ; not yet that soul
Heroic goes to its reward. He lives.
But higher, higher mount the pæans wild
Of foemen, loud proclaiming victory,
And with the shouts the trumpet harshly blends.
Now, now, in very truth his hour is come !
He falls, and o'er his lowly, senseless form
A score of arms upraise the murderous spear ;
Death aims his grisly dart ! But suddenly,
With warning gesture, one springs in the midst
That cries, —
    " Forbear, forbear, and harm him not !
Who doeth Damon injury shall die.
I, Dionysius, give command that he,
In double irons, under treble guard,

Shall straight be taken to the prison-house
Of gloomy Lithotomiæ, and there
Securely be confined.

     "And when three days
Are past, and on the last hath come the set
Of sun, he shall be brought unto this place,
Where publicly the city may look on,
To be beheaded, as a sign to all
That I alone am lord of Syracuse.

"Such is my will and pleasure. Make ye haste
And bear him hence.

     "As to the rest who live,
They have my pardon."

      Thus the night doth end.
For now, above the ocean-floor, the east
Is kindling with the ruddy flakes that paint
The early summer morn.

CANTO III.

ARGUMENT.

PYTHAGORAS. — Meeting of the Pythagorean Brotherhood of Syracuse. Alethes speaks. Lycidas returns from Lithotomiæ and relates the particulars of an interview between Damon and Dionysius. The tyrant will release the captive if any one will wear his chains as a hostage to insure his return before the time fixed for his execution. Many of the Brothers seek to assume this suretyship, but at last yield to Pythias. — Ortygia: Interview between Pythias and the tyrant; Pythias obtains the required permission to become Damon's hostage. — Lithotomiæ: Interview between Damon, Pythias, and Philistus; Damon is forced very unwillingly to leave Pythias in his stead. — Irené, the home of Damon. Interview between Damon and Calanthe, his wife; Damon bids her a last farewell and departs on his return to Syracuse. — Pythias at the block. Damon returns just in time to save his friend. The tyrant, struck with admiration, releases both, and asks to be taken as a third member of their fellowship.

I.

PYTHAGORAS![1] the mighty flow of æons yet to come,
Fulfilling Time, which, like the last of heavenly
    spheres, enwraps

---

[1] See Appendix E.

All things, shall not outlive thy fame. More 'during than the bronze
Of regal monuments, and loftier than the pyramids,
Thy glory shall remain and be renewed in endless growth.

What though by Metapontum's strand [1] the envious sea invade
The land, unyielding keeper of thy tomb and of the dust
That was thy mortal part? The subtile chariot of the soul
Hath sped afar to fields Elysian where the good and purified,
Beyond corruption and the power of death, are clothed upon
With immortality and made like Him whom worlds obey.
Most noble was thy life's reward, illustrious the prize.

Fair Samos, rising in queen-like beauty from the Ægean wave,
Renowned in commerce and the arts, gave unto Hera birth;

---

[1] The tomb of Pythagoras at Metapontum was to be seen as late as the time of Cicero.

But not the goddess lends thy native isle a greater
    meed
Of honor than dost thou, whose name now fills the
    universe.

Blind follies, grovelling passions were for others, not
    for thee.
That mystic letter[1] from whose stem diverge to either
    side
Twin branches, was to thee a symbol of the ways of
    life,
Of Virtue and of Vice. The steep and narrow path
    that mounts
Upon the right remained thy choice until the goal
    was won.

The boundaries of time and space which fetter mortal
    man

---

[1] The letter Y was the Pythagorean symbol of human life. Early youth, before the moral character is formed, is represented by the stem, the right branch is the path of virtue, the left the broader path of vice. Virgil may have had in view this Pythagorean type when he wrote. —

"Hic locus est, partes ubi se via findit in ambas:
Dextera quae Ditis magni sub moenia tendit;
Hac iter Elysium nobis; at laeva malorum
Exercet poenas, et ad impia Tartara mittit."
                                    Æn. VI, 540.

By the Stoics, virtue was represented by a straight line, the vices by curves.

Could ill confine thy footsteps and the soaring of a mind
That, far surpassing earthly knowledge, strove to reave the sky
Of all its treasured secrets, cosmic order to unfold,
And nearer to approach the One Ineffable who is
Whatever is or hath been or shall be forevermore.[1]

The hidden learning of the nations was sought out by thee,
And from the revelation, Wisdom, Strength, and Beauty sprang,
And blending in harmonious presence, did thy being fill.
Thy wandering footsteps strayed where Nilus rolls his yellow tide,
The bald skull of the desert mocks the heavens' changeless eye,
And Memnon's statue[2] greets with tuneful chord the rays of morn;

---

[1] An inscription on the ancient temple of Neïth, — the Egyptian Minerva, — at Saïs, a city of the Egyptian Delta, ran as follows: "I am the things that have been, and that are, and that will be; and no mortal has ever yet taken off the veil that covers me; the fruit which I brought forth became the Sun."

[2] In the temple of Serapis, at Thebes, stood a colossal statue of Memnon, which gave forth harmonious sounds when it received the rays of the rising sun. The ruins of this statue still remain. The sound has been explained by a physical cause analogous to that which produces the acoustic phenomenon of the Æolian harp.

And where afar upon Euphrates' banks uprise the walls
Of royal Babylon, and where Judæa's sons, restored
From wandering, renewed the temple that their fathers built;
And from the moaning Bosporus unto far Calpe's bound.
Unveiled to thee were Delphic and Idæan mysteries,
The lore of magi and the *adyta* of sacred things;
Mankind thy coming hailed where'er dispersed throughout the earth;
"I greet thee," and "God speed thee." were thy welcome and farewell.
Thus sought the world to make its wisdom thine, that as thou wast
Of all first called "Philosopher," so mightst thou be the chief.

There rose within the clear illumination of thy mind
A vision of the Architect Divine, whose thought alone,
In long-lost æons past, had formed the bright celestial throng
That minister to Him, had kindled evening's gilded train,
And purple morn, had set in space the ponderous globes of Earth
And Counter-Earth, the sunlit moon and all the heavenly spheres,

That, with a harmony too pure for human sense, revolve
Around their unseen central-fire, the flaming Tower of Zeus.[1]

In this theophany didst thou behold a Highest Good,
Eternal, infinite, unchangeable. To thee it told
Of an Omniscient Mind, an Arm Omnipotent that guides
The universe, an Omnipresent Eye, whose constant gaze
Doth ever view each inmost secret of the heart's recess.
And since creation from Essential Goodness had emerged,
Informed by perfect power and wisdom immanent in Him,
Its every part was rightly made as best for our estate.

And thou hast taught that as true happiness cometh of Him,
The Source of Good, so toward Him both our thoughts and deeds should tend, —
That we should pay high honor to His name and to His oath,
And in all rightful undertakings early seek His aid.

---

[1] See Appendix E.

To thy well-ordered vision, freed from earthly dross,
    and pure,
Had He revealed each shining orb that in the firmament
Of Virtue rolls majestic and eternal round His throne,
To such unchangeable and sacred guidance didst thou
    point,
That by its aid our souls might sooner mount to endless bliss.

Thou, thou of all men, best hast taught what meaneth
    Brotherhood;
And from the great impression of thy mind thy votaries
Have gained new bonds of sympathy and love, and
    to the world
Displayed grand deeds of high and noble and illustrious worth.
No longer may thy chosen Fellowship behold thee here,
But still our souls reflect thine imaged presence and
    thy words.
Nor mourn we wisely; for thy being, as thy fame,
    doth now
Surmount the earth and tower amid the star-decked
    canopy.

II.

Near by preserving Fortune's marbled fane
Were met within their place of gathering

Our Brotherhood of Syracuse. But far
To seek were most of those who clasped our hands
In fellowship in happier days. Alas!
'Neath Gela's walls the hostile spear had freed
Full many a soul from earth's dark prison-house,
And left us naught but envy of such fate;
And on the morn when Freedom winged her flight,
Of those who, timely warned, returned to die —
If so their country bade — a freeman's death,
The living told the multitude of slain;
And of the living heroes of that strife
None was who mourned not to survive his wounds.

Sad was our convocation. Hour like this
Had never gloomed upon our fatherland,
Nor on the welfare of our Brotherhood.
Yet faithful to the steadfast tie that binds
In loyalty our esoteric band,
Each true to each and to our Fellowship,
The place of our resort had promptly gained;
And while without the clouds more darkly frowned,
Unto our upturned gaze more brightly gleamed
The symbol of that mystic, sacred Fount,
Whence Nature, as our Order, draws her life.[1]

---

[1] Reference is here made to the *tetractys* (in Greek, Τετρακτύς, *the number four*), which, to the Pythagoreans, symbolized the fount of ever-flowing life and being (παγὰν ἀενάου φύσεως. *Carm. Aur.*, 48). Upon this symbol the Pythagoreans took a certain

Here might we find a refuge from the storm,
And, touched with mutual pity, comfort seek,
Or, in commingled grief, lament the dead!

To meet each friendly grasp, each fond embrace,
Lo! last of all, came Pythias. Braver knight
Than he ne'er trod the battle field; more true
Had ne'er partaken of our mysteries.
From where the slain lay thick our loving arms
Had borne him tenderly. The refluent tide
Of life returned; and now, with feebler step,
He came once more to greet the Sons of Light,
And, as none other, welcome from them take.
Yet scars of cruel wounds remained, fell proof
How great the miracle that saved from death
Him, the chief hero of that fatal morn.

III.

All were attentive as Alethes rose
And said, responding to the thoughts of all, —

---

oath, of which the fragment given us by Jamblichus, in his Life of Pythagoras, has been rendered as follows: —

> "By that pure, quadrilat'ral name on high,
> Nature's eternal fountain and supply,
> The parent of all souls that living be, —
> By it, with faithful oath, I swear to thee."

"Brothers, once more within these peaceful walls,
Where dwell Light, Love, and Truth, the living meet.
But not with joy returns this social hour;
Deep in the depths of sorrow mourns each heart.

"No longer may we share the polity
Which, under equal laws and equal rights,
Made each within the city peer of each.
Nor longer will the ægis of the free,
Forth flashing terror, as the fabled shield
Of Zeus, unite us 'gainst the savage foe.

"Fallen and helpless lies the commonwealth!
A tyrant's will stands for the people's rule,
And with him are our fortunes and our lives.

"Nor this alone. The unavailing tear
Will often flow in memory of those
Who fell so nobly in our latest strife.
Too manly to endure a despot's frown,
Too patriotic to survive the State,
They gave themselves in willing sacrifice,
Whereof the glory may assuage our woe.

"But when will end our longing and our grief
For the dear friends among our Brotherhood,
Who, not by alien hands, have passed away?
The fratricidal steel that shed their blood

Brought ruin to the nation, and to us
Perpetual sorrow for the untimely dead.
For these we mourn as only Brothers may.
No more will their glad footsteps find this place
Of wonted gathering. No more with them
May we conjoin within these walls as once,
In holy offices of Love and Truth,
Of Friendship, Charity, Benevolence.

" Yet there they sank to rest where for mankind
'T is glorious to die.
                    " So may kind Earth
Take fondly to her bosom that which sprang
From Earth, whilst in the realm above both Joy
And Immortality their souls inwreath.

" And is now filled the measure of our ills,
Ingathered is the harvesting of death?

" Alas! still one remains his doom to meet:
With fetters bound, deep in the quarried depths
Of Lithotomiæ, Damon captive lies, —
Of rank sublime among the Brotherhood,
The chosen leader of our Fellowship.

" The tyrant hath condemned him that he die
To-morrow ere depart the beams of day.
Would we might save his life! But hope seems vain,

As vain have been our efforts in the past.
The tyrant will give ear to none. With mind
Firm fixed in his fell purpose, he is deaf
To such as speak of mercy. He declares
That die our Brother must and shall, as now
Appointed.
    "Yet for counsel are we met,
Each lending aid to each, that we may learn,
If haply new endeavor may avail
To rescue Damon from his threatened fate.

" Grand is the mystery of Brotherhood,
That binds us each to each! An orb it shines,
With beams eternal, pure, of Light and Life
And Love, to help us in our journeying on
And upward to the realms of endless day,
Where, in communion sweet, beneath the Eye
Divine, earth's labor o'er, the harvest reaped,
Our souls shall find repose.
     " The outer world
Knows not the guiding-star that lights our path ;
Unveiled to us, it knits in unity,
And, hand to hand and heart to heart, conjoins
Our Fellowship till time shall be no more.
The sundering sea cannot divide our love,
Nor fleeting years nor Death's fell stroke destroy.
The centuries may waste the monuments
That mark the pride, the pageantry of man ;

The firm, unshaken earth, the mountain-tops
That rest amid the clouds, may find a grave
Beneath the encroaching surges of the deep;
Yet still shall Friendship's mystic tie unite,
And still the light that guides our Brotherhood,
Kindled by torch of heavenly flame, burn bright.
Art thou our Brother? Then thou wear'st a crown
More proud than any kingly potentate;
For thou art of that band whose loyalty
To thee, as thine to them, can never fail.
Does lying slander harm thee? Every tongue
Shall strive to keep unsullied thy repute.
Does sickness waste thee? Thou shalt find in us
The willing ministrants to thy relief.
Does danger threaten? Knowing this, we give
Thee timely warning that thou mayst avoid.
Has death encompassed thee? With fortitude
Would we imperil life to save thine own.

" Such is our Brotherhood, and such the love
That makes a Brother but our ' other self.'[1]

---

[1] This conforms to Pythagoras' definition of a friend, — ἐστὶ γὰρ ὥς φαμεν ὁ φίλος δεύτερος ἐγώ.

Another Pythagorean definition of friendship was, "Two bodies, — one soul," — σώματα μὲν δύο ψύχη δὲ μία. A friend was "half of the soul," — ἥμισυ τῆς ψυχῆς.

Horace employs the last definition in an ode addressed to his friend and patron, Mæcenas: —

DAMON AND PYTHIAS.

Then with a common purpose let us seek,
If haply Damon may escape his doom.
Let each make known what seemeth to him best.
Erelong will friendly Lycidas return.
Who to the prison went charged with our love
For Damon, and right well provided, too,
With gold, most potent to unloose the tongues
Of surly jailers and to gain us tidings."

IV.

These words Alethes spake, and suddenly,
As if in answer to the heart's desire,
Into our presence Lycidas returned.
Welcomed by all, an audience he claimed,
And thus related to us what we sought: —
"Brothers, with eager steps I hastened hence

"Ah te meae si partem animae rapit
Maturior vis, quid moror altera,
Nec carus aeque nec superstes
Integer?"

Od. II, XVII, 5.

And again, in an ode addressed to the ship that was carrying his friend Virgil, the poet, to Greece: —

"Navis, quae tibi creditum
Debes Virgilium finibus Atticis
Reddas incolumem precor,
Et serves animae dimidium meae."

Od. I, III, 5.

And gained admission to the prison-house
Of Lithotomiæ. Within its gloom
I strove with unavailing prayers to reach
The cell of Damon. Neither gold nor tears
Could overcome the tyrant's stern command
Imposed upon the keepers, that alone
Our Brother should await the hour of death.
Thus had my errand almost fruitless been.
But one Damœtas, who kept guard within
And seemed to have compassion for our friend,
Most willingly, for he refused reward,
Yet secretly acquainted me of this
I now repeat as he hath given it.

" 'T was yesterday that some unknown desire
Or fancy led the tyrant to the cell
Of Damon. With him were his satellites,
Philistus and those other sycophants
Who share the honors of his new-made power.
Subservient to imperial state, the guard
Quickly unclosed the ponderous barriers
And lighted him into the dungeon's depths.
There he beheld the captive, doubly ironed
And feeble from his wounds.
                            " Then unto him
The tyrant said, ' Well mayst thou now regret
Thy folly on the night when thou mad'st bold
To face my power. Ay, suppliant at my feet,
Implore forgiveness! Hast thou aught to say?'

" And Damon answered, 'I have no regret
Save for my country; and I dread thee not,
That I should ask for mercy. As thou wilt,
Release me from these chains or take my life.'

"'Thou hast no fear of death?'
        "'I fear it not.
Against the foe and at the latest hour
I perilled all for freedom. This now lost,
Death seems more welcome than to live a slave.'

"'Thy friends, the members of thy Brotherhood,
Are striving all to save thee; they entreat
Most earnestly that thy life may be spared.'

"'Ah, Dionysius, never canst thou know
The tie that binds them to me! Hath my fate
Then caused such sorrow? From my prison-house
My heart goes out to them in thankfulness.
Faithful are these amid earth's darkest ills.
Had I of one brief hour the boon, forthwith
Would I haste unto them to say farewell.
It may not be. Still shall we meet again
In time to come.'
      "'Thou speakest mysteries.
But liveth there none other whom ere death
Thou wouldst revisit? Is there none, save these,
Of whom thou wouldst eternal parting take?
Hast thou a wife or child?'"

"'Forbear, forbear,
Most cruel Dionysius! Make for me
New instruments of pain, prolong my life
Beneath a quivering, an unceasing flow
Of anguish; rack and torture as thou wilt,
And men shall hear me with my latest breath
Defy thy might. But spare this pang, and speak
No more, no more of those whom thou hast named!
Oh, could I steel myself against the thought
Of all most maddening, that the fatal day
Will come ere I again may see their forms.
As purest star hath risen 'mid this gloom
The beauteous vision of my far-off home,
Of wife and child. And ever in my dreams
An image of the loved ones calms my rest.
Yet would my reason wander from its throne
Had I no respite from the dreadful thought
Of separation. But the cruel words
From thee, the author of the woe that frets
My soul, renew this grief with keenest pang.
Once more I seem to gaze on her who waits
With fond embrace my coming, and the joy
Of our fair child, half told in prattling speech
To us whose mutual love she binds anew.
Oh, mayst thou, Dionysius, deign to grant
To me, most wretched, but a single day
To seek my home, a last farewell to say!
Then will I swift return and suffer death.'

DAMON AND PYTHIAS.

"' So, Damon, have I moved thy lofty soul,
Now cravest thou the favor of my power!
Yet should I grant the boon thou hast besought,
Canst give assurance of thy coming back
To meet thy doom?' 'Thou 'lt have the very best.'
'Then hast thou gold?' 'Not gold have I, but that
Which gold shall never taint, — an honest word.
That will I pledge as gage of my return.'
'Can I believe thy promise would avail
Against the love of life? Not so wilt thou
Escape me and the headsman! But dost think, —
Thou 'lt laugh, Philistus, at the merry jest, —
Dost think there lives among thy Brotherhood
A Brother who would aid thee in thy stress,
Here wear thy chains, awaiting thy return,
To die instead of thee, shouldst thou not come
Within the time appointed?'
      "'Ay! not one,
But all, O Dionysius, willingly
Would help me thus if they but knew my need;
Yet would I suffer none so dear as these
To bear my chains or peril life for me.'
'What folly hast thou babbled to the winds,
If I have heard thy words! Then hast thou faith
Thy Brotherhood would peril life for thee?'
'So have I said, O Dionysius; so
Once more I tell thee.'
      "'Damon, hopest thou

By this asseveration to commend
Such marvel unto our belief ? Vain, vain
The effort! What the mysteries may be
Of those among thy Order, what the oaths
And mutual duties of their fellowship
I care not. For I well and truly know
That not in Syracuse nor in the land
Can one be found who, willingly, would leave
The bloom and beauty of the outer world,
With all that makes the happiness of life,
And here, within these gloomy, noisome depths,
Put on thy chains, and as a pledge for thee,
Await the coming of the dreadful hour.
If such there were, then would I grant thy prayer.

" ' But time is swiftly speeding. Let us haste,
Philistus, for the moment is near by
When I must mount my throne in regal state,
And hold my court. And, Damon, as to thee ' —

" ' I go, thou tyrant, to a glorious death!' "

V.

When Lycidas had ended, straight there rose
The murmurings of wonder and of joy.
And then, as if by common impulse moved
To friendly strife, each Brother sought to be

The foremost in his offering to haste
To Dionysius, and of him beg leave
To be a pledge for Damon's prompt return.

Whilst all in worthy emulation strove,
And harmony was lost in that wherein
Each close agreed with each, none might prevail.
At last, in silence, we gave willing ear
To Pythias, who was Damon's dearest friend.

" Brothers," he said, " I thank you that I may
Be heard, in claiming that which to myself
Peculiarly belongs ; for not alone
The common tie which binds our fellowship
Impels me, though the same might well suffice
At such a time ; for Friendship is our first
And grandest bond. Another right is mine,
That Damon should accept me as his pledge.
In early childhood's hours began my love
For him.   Fond memory hath oft restored
The petty hamlet 'mid Sicilian hills,
Its cottages half hidden by the wealth
Of nature's bloom, where passed our early life
In sweet companionship.   Again I seem
To mingle with him in the jocund sports
That swiftly sped the shining days of youth,
And in the tasks wherein, with minds as one,
We conned the mysteries of things unknown.

E'en then was Damon, as in after-time,
My best and firmest friend, the soul of truth
And honor; pure, heroic, masterful,
Exemplar of his boyish following.
And as the tranquil river's peaceful flow,
Calmly moved on the current of our joys.

" But suddenly, ere we had sprung to manhood,
The call of perilled country summoned us
To leave our pleasant home for other scenes
More mighty than our land had yet beheld.
We came to Syracuse. And soon began
The grand, ensanguined drama of that siege,
Wherein the armament of Athens strove
With sword and spear to pass the rampired walls
Our city to o'erwhelm. Then side by side
We faced the foe. E'en from the day when gleamed
Over the ocean-floor their thousand sails
Until the last, when Victory placed her crown
Of gold upon our City's brow, our lives,
Our hopes were one. But oft in peril were
Our lives, and thrice when danger imminent
That threatened instant death, assailed mine own,
The friendly arm of Damon came to save.

" Then was our mutual love still firmer knit
On other battle-fields; and when erelong,
The tie of Brotherhood had made more pure

And sacred that which bound our hearts before,
In very truth was each to each the half
Of his own soul.[1]
                "At Acragas we fought,
And there, once more, upon the dreadful night
When all the countless population swarmed
In terror from the doom that overhung
The fated town, my life was saved by him.
And at the final hour, when Prudence marked
The scheme of treason, now, alas! fulfilled,
Together we marched forth in the proud host
That Dionysius led to Gela's aid.
But vain our going! Sad the day of hope
We left our homes to seek Geloan walls!
A mightier foe than Lybia's swarthy ranks
Was nigh. Men knew it not; or if by us
Forewarned, they heeded not, until uprose
In hideous gloom, yet full revealed by Proof,
Whose trembling torch flamed at the hour of fate,
The treason that hath wrecked our commonwealth.
'Twas then, with such as were of all our knights
Most true, we sprang in haste upon our steeds
And, as an arrow, passed the ghostly throngs
That filled the roads, and sped to save the State.
Alas, its doom was sealed! The smoking void
Of Achradina's gate, the blood-stained earth,

---

[1] See preceding note, page 78.

The relics of the slain, proclaimed the end
Of Syracusan freedom.
      " From the dead
I rose; yet death seemed blissful to the woe
That after came when Damon's fate was told.
Then, broken-hearted, reft of country, friend,
This firm resolve I made: that if my life,
So oft preserved by him, might save his own,
It should be given in willing sacrifice.

" Brothers, my tale is told; and judge ye now
If any hath a better right than mine
To wear the chains of Damon. I it is
Who was his earliest friend. To him I owe
My life and all the years of happiness
Of which he was the giver and the source.
Oppose me not, my Brothers, for with mind
As firm in this as in its love for him,
I justly take upon myself forthwith
To seek the tyrant's court, and there obtain
Fulfilment of my heart's inmost desire.
The hour is nigh when Dionysius, robed
In royal splendor, will ascend his throne
And there, in novel power, receive the prayers
And plaints of those who need imperial aid.
Such is the proclamation.
      " Then, farewell!
Farewell, dear Brothers, till we meet again."

He ended, none opposing, and 'mid tears
And hearty " God speed ! " vanished from our sight.

VI.

Where stands Ortygia's stately citadel,
A fortress and a palace, was the home
Of Dionysius. Towers and battled walls,
Which gleamed in strength and beauty far o'er land
And sea, there made secure his royal sway.
As shadows, ever round his footsteps thronged,
By day and night, a mercenary horde
Of Syracusans and Italiotes.
Their duty 't was his slightest wish to heed,
And guard from harm his person and his throne.
None might approach his presence unannounced,
Save only those, his friends and parasites,
Whose loyalty was proved. Yet, in the pride
Of kingly rule unfelt before, by act
Of public proclamation, had he deigned
To grant imperial leave that whoso would
Might daily seek him, at a stated hour,
And humbly make petition to be heard.
And thus it was upon the day whose flight
Should yield to that when Damon was to die,
Within his audience-hall the tyrant sat
And listened to the supplications made.
Philistus was beside him, and hard by

The rake and spendthrift Hipparinus stood,
With other courtiers, whose old-time repute
Was evidential of their welcome here.
While sheathed in glittering helmet, cuirass, greaves,
With sword and spear and shield, each guardsman held
His station near the footstool of the throne.

Now when already many had besought
The tyrant for his aid, or homage paid
To him as ruling monarch of the State,
Philetor, keeper of the inner gate,
Approached, obsequious, and, with lowly bow,
Announced, "O sovereign, there is one who begs
That I admit him to thy presence, known
To be most hostile to thy power.
                                    "He hath,
We fear, intent of evil; for he would
In no wise hint the purpose of his mind."
And Dionysius said, "Whate'er he seek,
Forbid not that he enter. Let my guard
With watchful eye observe him."
                                    Then within
Came Pythias, and awaited leave to speak.

"What, Pythias! leader of my bitterest foes!
Thou hast an iron heart to venture here!
Fain would I tell my guard to cleave thee where

Thou standest; but the pardon late decreed
Doth shield thee. Rumor had pronounced thee dead.
Thou liv'st to see me king! Why cam'st thou here?"
" In hope to loose a Brother from his chains."
" Who is that Brother?" " Damon." "And what
 wouldst?"
" Myself to offer in his stead, that he,
Before the hour appointed for his death,
May look on wife and child. So should not he
Return, on me shall fall the headsman's stroke."

" What madness, what delirium do I hear?
Thou knowest not nor canst what thou hast sought."

" O Sovereign, in the soberness of truth,
My lips reveal to thee my heart's desire."

" Then tell me yet again what thou wouldst have."

" That till the hour when Damon is to die,
He may be free and I may wear his bonds, —
My life to be the price of his default."

" Amazement wild confounds me! Can it be
That such a wonder will command belief?
Recallest thou, Philistus, how, in vain,
The lips of Damon late averred the same,
That hath fulfilment here most marvellous?

Yet Pythias hath not seen his captive friend.
It matters not.
    " But tell me, ere thy prayer
Be granted or refused, hast thou not heard
That Damon languishes 'neath ponderous chains,
Amid thick gloom, wherein no ray of light
Can shine? Or thus forewarned, dost yet desire
His sufferings to take upon thyself?"

" Thy words, O Dionysius, urge me on
With swifter speed to seek his prison-house."

" Yet shouldst thou, as a pledge of his return,
Await in vain his coming, thinkest thou
The headsman's sword shall loiter in its task?
Dost hope my mercy will relent at last
To save thee from destruction self-imposed?"

" Naught could I hope of mercy, should he fail.
But fail he will not. Might I dream of that,
More welcome were his chains, — most welcome,
  death!"

" Amazement ever greater doth enwrap
My soul!
   " But tell, what's Damon unto thee,
That thou, in his relief, wouldst venture life?"

"He is a Brother, bound to me by ties
Which only those can feel on whom they rest."

"What tie can lead thee to imperil life?"

"A bond which so unites our Brotherhood
That none hath fear of peril, pain, or death,
When led by duty in a Brother's need."

"Think'st thou thy friend such risk would take for
 thee?"

"Greater, indeed, had he incurred for me
Ere this new bond of union made us one."

"But what assurance hast thou that again
Thou wouldst behold him whom thou hadst set free?"

"The sun is not more constant in his course
Than Damon in the path of honesty;
And linked with honor is his love for me,
And with our mutual love, those sacred ties,
Which, whoso well observes, can never err.
Yet would I hope he come not ere the hour,
So might my death release him from his doom."

"'T is wonderful! The proof of love like this,
Surpassing all that I had known before
Of friendship or had dreamed, hath filled my breast

With admiration, with astonishment!
Pythias, I grant thy prayer. But mark thou well,
The doom prepared for Damon waits for thee,
Should he return not ere the appointed time.
Thee, O Philistus, I permit to wear
This royal token of authority.
Take Pythias with thee and straightway repair
Unto the prison-house; at once remove
From Damon every bond, and set him free,
With knowledge of whate'er thou shouldst impart.
Let Pythias be confined in Damon's stead
And put in chains.
     " To-morrow we shall see —
For Damon goes forever from our sight —
How one can die that loveth so his friend."

VII.

" Oh, joyful hour! The wanderer hath returned.
Once more I gaze upon my beauteous home,
And feel the fond embrace of wife and child,
And press them to my heart. I live anew
In ecstasy of bliss ineffable!
But now, alas! whence comes such woful change?
All vanishes to naught, and where these were
I look for them in vain. What midnight gloom
Now thick enshroudeth me? What fetters bind?
'T was but an empty dream! Again I wake

Amid the darkness of my prison-house,
And the bright vision wrought in fancy's flight
Departs as to the dungeon-keep my soul
Returns. Oh, blessed image of my home!
Oh, sad awakening from its fleeting joys!
And shall death take me hence forevermore
Ere I behold the loved ones? Must they wait
In vain my coming, till the fearful hour
That tells them of my fate? May no last word
Of fondness, no farewell, assuage the grief
Of parting?
   "Terrible beyond all pangs
The fearful shrink from and the brave defy!
But for this thought my dauntless will should soar,
High-raised and triumphing, beyond this gloom,
These chains, and death itself! For what is death
To him that dies in such a cause? Let none
For me lament the fatal hour, or drop
The unavailing, the untimely tear.
I go to meet my doom with steadfast heart,
Sustained by hope, which giveth at the block
To every patriot forecast of the years
That are to come, when Freedom may regain
New life and being from the illustrious worth
Of such as nobly perished in her cause.
So shall I pass from life to be enshrined
Forevermore in immortality
With those who died that Freedom might survive.

"E'en now, methinks, draws near the longed-for hour;
The bolts are backward thrust; the massy door
Grates on its hinges. Yonder shines a ray
Piercing these depths where day and night are one.
Ay, hither comes Damœtas. He alone,
Of those appointed as my keepers here,
Hath seemed to have compassion for my lot.
And there's Philistus, Dionysius' friend.
There, too, with clanging arms, the prison-guard
That will attend me to the place of death.
But who in haste outstrippeth all the rest,
Who now enfolds me in this close embrace?"

"'T is Pythias, bringing life and liberty
And happiness! My Damon, thou art free!"

"Pythias, my Brother and my dearest friend!
I 've mourned for thee as numbered with the dead.
How have I longed to see thee ere the last!"

"And me thou now beholdest. Let me help
To loose the fetters from thee; they shall gall
Thy limbs and weigh thee to the earth no more.
From this eternal gloom thou shalt go forth
To gaze upon the sunlit hills and breathe
The fresh and fragrant air of heaven. Again
Wilt thou be welcomed by our Brotherhood,
And feel the twining arms of wife and child,

And in a life renewed taste bliss unfelt
Before.
  " At last thy sorrows find an end;
And now with joy my breast o'erflows that I,
Whom thou hast loved so well, may be the first
To tell the tidings and to set thee free.
All things are rightly cared for. Near the house
Of Calydon, our Brother, is thy steed,
Waiting to bear thee swiftly to thy home.
Now art thou bound no longer by these chains,
Now has thou license to depart. Farewell!
Farewell!"
  " Say'st thou farewell? What meanest thou?
Come quickly with me, Pythias! Let us hence!"

"Here, Damon, I remain; but linger not
For me."
  " Thou to remain within this cell!
What words are these, my Brother? Thinkest thou
I leave thee here?"
  " Here, Damon, must I stay;
Thus have I gained the royal leave that thou
Mayst to thy home return. The tyrant looks
For thee no more. Then hasten! I will here
Abide; for thee is life and liberty."

" Ah, Pythias, until now thou'st called me friend!
From childhood I have loved thee. In our joys,

Our griefs, were we as one. With equal steps,
Conjoined in hand and heart, have we pursued
Life's rugged path, and distant seemed the day
When either should forget the mutual claim
Of old-time friendship and of Brotherhood.
But, Pythias, thou hast known me not. Vain, vain
Have been the years which have united us,
When thou to me can proffer such dishonor.
Take back thy words and give me back my chains!
Kind though thy purpose, thou of all most dear,
Yet ne'er through me shalt thou endure these bonds.'

" Damon, my Brother, let my love for thee,
Well proven in the years that are gone by,
Make answer for me unto thy reproach;
And let the life thou hast so often saved,
E'en as it is thy boon, be thine to have
As the last offering Pythias can bestow.
Mine are the chains; for thee is liberty."

" Talk not to me of liberty, when gained
Through infamy! Again will I put on
These manacles, less grievous than the thought
That I could e'er be false to Friendship's tie."

" False thou couldst never be! But false were I
If, having come to save my best-loved friend,
My purpose should prove recreant to its trust,
Yielding to that which makes more just its aim."

"These words are useless; leave me to my fate!"

Then spake Philistus, "By the sovereign's charge,
On me imposed, thou, Damon, now art free,
And must depart forthwith. If then thou wilt,
When thou hast looked on wife and child, thou mayst
Return, and at the appointed hour meet death.
But shouldst thou, ere the hour, come not, thy friend,
Who hath obtained the royal leave to be
Imprisoned in thy stead, as gage for thee,
Must undergo thy sentence. Thou art free,
And he, my prisoner. To-morrow eve
Or thou or he must die."
       And Damon said,
"Dream'st thou, Philistus, I could thus forsake
A friend, a Brother, leaving him in gaol,
Captive for me, to meet with death should chance
Delay my coming?
     "Pythias, is it well
That in thy boundless love thou hast for me
Assumed such dreadful hazard? Nay! thyself
Carry my sad adieu to the sweet home
I nevermore may see, while here I wait
Not long the swift-approaching hour supreme,
The mortal stroke that brings, at last, repose."

Thereon Philistus, "Not with me it rests
In aught to change the sovereign's strict command;

By his imperial will, of whom I am
The trusty minister, go forth thou must,
But Pythias shall remain."

"Alas, alas!"
Cried Damon. "Cruel fate! Hadst thou, my friend,
Foreseen the anguish that now rends my breast!
Oh, that thy heart, too faithful to the last,
Had kept its generous purpose unrevealed!
Yet is there time. As me thou lovest, seek
The tyrant and thy heedless prayer recall!"
Then Pythias answered, " Hither have I come
In hope to save thy life. Nor words of thine,
Thou one best loved, nor fear of mortal pangs,
Can change the steadfast purpose of my soul.
In the lone dungeon's gloom I'll wear thy bonds
More proudly than the sovereign, on his throne
In state imperial, wears the kingly crown.
And on the morrow, at the set of sun,
Pythias for thee would die. O Damon, grant
Me this! Bear hence my last farewell,
And in the coming years sometimes recall
The friend whose latest prayer ascends for thee.
To wear thy chains, my Brother, e'en the least
Amongst our Fellowship aspired. To them,
As unto me, the voice of Duty spake
Imperiously when first was manifest
The means of helping thee in thy distress.
But when to me, thy friend of friends, alone,

Each Brother yielded up his rightful claim,
A grander purpose dawned within my soul
Than to assure thee respite for a day.
I thought to give thee freedom, life, and joy;
The pangs of death to suffer in thy stead;
To meet the noble lofty fate of him
That bravely perishes to save a friend.
I sought the tyrant. In amaze he heard,
Consented to my prayer. By his supreme
Authority I am thy hostage. But
For what? When he declared thou wouldst return
No more to Syracuse, my former hope
More brightly burned to light me on my way
To gain thy dungeon and fulfil its aim.
I thought of loved ones far away; but these
Had mourned for me ere now, except thy arm
Had rescued me. As from the glorious beams
Of day I passed, all nature, wreathed in smiles
Alluring, beckoned unto me to stay
My steps; but clearer shone the guiding-star
That led me on. My vision gazed on thee
Alone, the object of my hope. In thee
I saw the friend who ofttimes had preserved
My life, — the joy, the pride, the chosen chief,
The loved and honored of our Brotherhood;
The father of a child within whose orbs
The morning beams of heavenly radiance play
Whene'er, with lisping tongue, she speaks thy name;

A husband, whose sad heart could have no grief
Surpassing that which unto earth would crush
Thy dear Calanthe in the fatal hour
Of revelation. Think of all, my friend,
For which thou livest! Well may I entreat
That I, not thou, may bear the mortal stroke.
Yet, since Philistus hath to thee disclosed
That which my tongue would ever have concealed,
Grant me at least this prayer. Refuse it not!
Speed to thy home this night! Behold thy wife,
Thy child! And then may God fulfil the hope
Thou mayst return to Syracuse no more.
It is ordained that now thou must depart.
But speak, and ere thy going let me rest
Assured that thou wilt straightway seek thy home."

" Pythias, I grant thy latest prayer. To-night
I hasten — oh, how mournfully! — to say
The parting word 'Farewell' to wife and child;
And on the morrow I return to meet
My doom. May God preserve thee till I come
Again!"
            One fond embrace, and so they parted.
The ponderous prison-door closed on the tomb
Where Pythias lay.
            Then from the gloomy depths
Did Damon, sorrowful in heart, come forth
And gaze upon a world of beauty, seen

In fading splendor 'neath the golden bars
Of parting day.

VIII.

The day is nigh; and through Irené's[1] glades
And 'mid the whispering leafage slowly creep
The forms uncouth of Darkness and of Night,
Who ever shrink, and, like as guilty things,
Pale at the first faint kindling of the dawn.

Not yet the cold, dank, earth-born shadows lift;
But eastward, in the dusky vault, the lamps
Of heaven now burn with feebler ray; and low
Adown, upon a pearl-white field, doth glow,
In dimly umbered hue, the morning-red.
The foul, gross airs, in swifter, swifter flight,
Are fleeting from the incense-laden breath
Of Her whose kindly murmuring e'er in love
Foretells to every drooping, trembling flower
The coming of the shining, joyous Hours.

Soon, one by one, the waning stars are quenched;
And where the dayspring draweth near, great waves
Of ruddy light empurple the bluey sky

---

[1] Irené, the home of Damon. Irené was the Goddess of Peace.

In ever-broadening, ever-brighter flow.
As now emerges out of ebbing gloom
The rock-ribbed, giant form of Ætna's mount,
Its flames decay, and from its molten depths
No longer the Cyclopian forges burn
To heaven their sickly fires.
      Through endless change
The dim auroral flushing is become
A saffron sea, whose sheeny line of surf
Swift mounts, and ever toward the zenith sweeps,
Until, slow cleaving ocean's iron-blue rim,
In splendor and in majesty enrobed,
The God of Day begins his mighty course.

Now Nature liveth in a life renewed;
And on green field and purple, vine-clad hill,
On whispering forest and low-murmuring brook,
Hyperion doth fling his golden shafts,
To gild with brighter hues the blooming earth,
Long roseate with the tints of crimson morn.

What wealth of happiness now fills thy realm,
Irené!
   From the smiling greensward, decked
With blossoms dew-besprent, to where thy groves
Re-echo from unseen, aërial bowers,
The liquid warbling of their painted choirs, —
All, all is joy.

Far, far away mounts up
To heaven the smoke of burning cities,
And flashing steel reflects the rays of morn.
Within thy peaceful bounds, nor sight nor sound
Disturbeth Love divine, as she conjoins
Harmonious Life and living Harmony,
With flowery fetters binding them in one.

Yet darkly, Home of Beauty, hath the sun
Of this bright day arisen unto her
Who, fairer than thyself, now cometh forth
From yonder cottage.
              Would her lonely heart
Swift flit on wings of love to seek its mate?
Erelong its inmost core shall feel such grief
As hopeth tearless rest from earthly ills,
Where flows the calm, Lethean flood of death.

Unto the margent cool her footsteps tend,
Where ofttimes she and Damon wont to watch
The distant flash of sail upon the sea,
The mirrored play of foliage in the stream
Below, the wide champaign, the western hills,
Robed in the splendor of declining day
Or tipt with morn's first beams.
                    And by her side
Anthera, tender image of the one
To whom she clingeth, ever stops to cull
Some bright-hued flower.

Together they repose
Them by the bank bedight with summer's bloom,
And there the mother, from the floral hoard
The child hath gathered, makes with loving hands
A garland for her nestling.
     "Would that now
Thy father might behold thee, little maid,"
She says, and places on her head the wreath,
With fond maternal care.
     And thus adorned,
Anthera, prattling, ever joyous, fills
The vocal air with childlike happiness,
And cheers the mother's breast.
     More swiftly fly
The blissful moments of the golden morn.
The streamlet's crystal flow, the smiling earth,
The blithesome song of birds from every spray,
Reflect a sunlight always brighter made
Within the lorn one's heart.
     But list! a sound
Is heard afar like that of clattering hoofs,
And ever nearer, clearer is it borne.
Who spurreth onward in so furious haste?
What joy or fear disturbs the mother's soul
That she so quickly hastes to clasp her child,
Gazing with earnest vision toward yon glade
Where first the unseen comer may be known?
Her doubt is for a moment; then she cries,

"'T is he! 'T is he!" And on his bounding steed
Her Damon, pale as death, flies to her side,
And, trembling, wraps her in a close embrace.

"My husband, might I utter half my heart
Would tell thee! Oh, what happiness before
Unfelt now gilds the radiant morn! Each tear
Since thy departure I have shed for thee,
As every prayerful sigh for thy return,
Hath made more glad the moment when I dwell
Upon thy ever-faithful breast in peace.
No cloud now dims the sky; more balmy breathes
The air; around me heaven and earth are robed
In brighter hues, and joy will be complete
When thou hast promised to depart no more."

"Beloved Calanthe, spare a heart distraught
By woe whereof thou ne'er hast dreamed! And Thou,
Great Power, uphold me with immortal strength!"

"What mean thy words, my Damon? Thou art pale,
Wayworn; but now mayst thou repose. Come sit
Thou here where we 've so oft reclined in days
Gone by; and take Anthera to thy arms.
Strange that thou hast not yet embraced thy child!
A blushing wreath she wears for thy return."

"Calanthe, unto thee my being flows;
For thou alone must deeply drink the cup

Of anguish when at last my tale is told.
Yet from the revelation I must make,
My soul shrinks back as from abysmal depths."

"An unknown terror, Damon, hast thou wrought
Within my breast! What mean thy dismal words?"

"Calanthe, I have ever loved thee; ay!
More than too eager tongue in speech can tell;
But have I always been to thee what thou
In hopefulness mad'st prayer for when the bay
And ivy blended on our nuptial eve?"

"More hast thou been to me. Those early dreams
But dimly shadowed forth my future joy.
I knew not then, as now, thy honor, faith,
And boundless love. The Hymenean song,
Calm rising in that mellow summer eve,
And softly-breathing Lydian flute, foretold
Of happiness, but not of such as I
Have felt with thee."
    "Calanthe, steel thy soul
To that I shall reveal! This day must I
Depart from home, from wife and child, to see
Them nevermore. No more! Oh, bitterness!
No more, no more!"
    "Oh, Damon, frightful are
Thy words! In mercy, speak to me and lift

This dreadful burden! All my heart's warm blood
Is ice!"

"May God support thee while I tell
The awful tidings thou must hear! Our State
Has been o'erthrown. The leader of our arms,
One Dionysius, has by force acquired
Despotic power, and now as tyrant rules.
Forewarned, I sought with others to defend
Our perilled fatherland from treason's grasp;
And hoping death or victory might betide,
Resistance made most vainly till the last.
'T was then, o'erwhelmed by numbers, I was borne
In chains to Lithotomiæ, there to be
Confined until the set of this day's sun,
When, by the tyrant's strict command, I must
Come forth into the Agora, to die."

"But thou art free! Thou hast escaped thy doom!
Thy chains no longer bind! A ray of joy
Now shines within my soul. Oh, let us haste!
With fair Anthera, let us seek afar
Some home as bright as this, where nevermore
May come the battle-sound or that dread word,
'Farewell!' Italia, or the distant East,
Or that blest clime beyond the boreal realm,[1]

---

[1] The Hyperboreans were supposed to dwell in the remote regions of the North, and to be a happy race, free from old age, disease, and war.

Shall be our place of refuge. There we'll live
A life that knows no sorrow. Wife and child
Will let thee wander from their side no more."

"Alas, Calanthe! that fond dream of love
And hope shall swiftly vanish as it dawned:
And even as thy soul is filled with faith
And honor, thou shalt read the fatal truth,
That not more surely comes the set of sun
Than Damon goes to meet the headsman's stroke.
Calanthe, as a pledge of my return
Within the appointed time, a dearest friend,
A Brother, wears my chains and perils life.
For unto Pythias, whom thou knowest well,
The tyrant gave consent that I once more
Might seek my home to say the parting word;
He to remain instead, and suffer death
In my default. Thus am I firmly bound
By tie more powerful than my prison bonds."

As when some mother-bird, that near her young,
Amid the enchanted foliage, swift outpours,
In endless flow of sweetness, all the joy
And sunshine of her heart, and so doth fill
The echoing grove with heavenly harmony, —
Pierced by the cruel archer's fatal shaft,
Yields up her little life, and suddenly
Her voice is still, and tiny nestlings call

In vain, in vain, — so, when Calanthe hears
The words foretelling Damon's doom, her soul
All-moanful sinks to silent, lonely depths,
Where mortal pain and sorrow can no more.

The silvery streamlet, gently gliding by,
The zephyr whispering 'mid o'erhanging boughs,
The warbled strains that float through chequered
        shade,
Nor e'en the child, which not unwittingly
Clingeth unto the mother's side and weeps, —
The garland fallen, scattered all its flowers, —
Can soothe Calanthe in this deadly grief,
Or rouse her from her husband's breast.
                                        The hour
Hath come, — the hour when manhood, honor, faith,
Are calling to the prison-house, the block,
The tomb! Crushed by o'ermastering woe, in vain
Doth Damon strive to say the parting word;
Too feebly do his lips respond.
                                        But time
Now urgeth, and Calanthe, hardly yet
Restored to life by many a fond caress,
Heareth the sad, half-uttered word, "Farewell!"
"Ah, stay!" she cries; "but for a little while
Be with thy wife and child!"
                                "A Brother's life,
Calanthe, is in peril whilst I wait.

Late was my coming, for, distraught by grief,
I wandered far from my accustomed path,
So must I hasten to return. The sun
Already mounteth high upon his course."

"Oh, Damon, that his setting might give me,
As thee, a grave! But for our child, my life
Should end with thine! The golden dreams that made
My future bright are gone forevermore.
Ah! what is left me now, forlorn of thee?
Dark is my path, and desolate! But not
Calanthe shall persuade thee to dishonor
Worse than death."
                        "O noble wife, these words
Lift up my soul! The anguish of this hour
Of separation seems to pass away,
And now I'll go with braver heart to bear
The mortal stroke. Farewell! farewell! Do thou
And sweet Anthera take from me a last
Embrace as pledge of my eternal love.
Forget me not in all the years to come.
A father and a husband ye will see
No more on earth! Yet knights, both true and tried,
Among my Brotherhood, will e'er provide
For you. Weep not, Calanthe! we shall meet
Again. Farewell! farewell!"
                              Upon his steed
Sprang Damon; and the mother, tear-bedimmed,

With trembling arms, held high her little one
To wave a last good-by.

IX.

What art thou, Death? The soul made vile by guilt
Doth fear thee as thou wert the chiefest ill;
And on the despot, whom thy watchful arm
Presseth in ever-swifter flight, thou fall'st
Like heaven's avenging bolt. But he, within
Whose sorrow-laden breast all hope is dead,
Welcomes the steel that cuts the thread of life,
And smiles when cometh near the hour supreme;
And patriotic hearts, on battle-field
And in the dungeon's midnight gloom, defy
Thy might; and all the good and wise, unmoved,
Await thy stroke. What art thou, then, O Death?
A shadow dim, a blessing or a curse,
Diversely taking from the souls of men
Thy form and nature.[1]
                    Through the flaming east,
As with the light of conflagration, shine
The beams of risen morn; and far away
The countless waves of dark-blue ocean smile,
And onward roll to seek yon fertile shore,

---

[1] After the Italian of Vincenzo Monti.

Whose waving leaves and opening flowers invite
To greet with blended joys the welcome day.
Ortygia's citadel and sea-girt walls
Gleam tall and white against the mounting orb,
And from the heights that crown Epipolæ
To where Anapus' flood glides on to pay
Its tribute to the main, all Syracuse
Is gladdened with the bright, celestial rays.

What throngs so early fill her streets? Why haste
So many to the market-place ere yet
Is come the wonted hour when Hermes [1] lifts
His golden wand? What novel cause hath brought
The multitudes, released from rustic toil,
That surge within the gates?
                              It is the day
When Damon is to die; and from afar
The bruited tidings of his mortal doom
Have drawn the greedy populace betimes,
Eager e'en now to view, with gaping mouth,
The ground erelong to redden with his blood.

---

[1] Hermes (Mercury) was the tutelary god of traffic. But this was only one of his many offices. He was also the messenger of the gods, the conductor of the dead, the god of all arts and sciences, and of peace; of prudence, cunning, fraud, and even of perjury; he was also, at least among the Romans, invoked by thieves. One of his epithets — χρυσόρραπις — referred to his bearing a golden rod with magical properties.

But while men gather, swift a rumor flies,
Believed by none, that Damon is released.
Yet soon confirmed, the wondrous tale is told
That Damon, by the sovereign's will set free,
Has gone from Syracuse to seek his home,
Leaving his friend in pledge of his return.
Amazement fills the souls of all. By what
Entreaty was the tyrant led to grant
This boon to Damon, who had, first and last,
Endeavor made to crush his traitorous scheme?
And stranger still, that Pythias, caring naught
For life, hath taken on himself the chains
Of Damon, with full knowledge thence should come
His own destruction! For who madly dreams
That Damon, now secure, and holding life
And liberty within his grasp, will e'er
Return to Syracuse? Such thoughts are thought
And uttered. And while some admire the hap
That gave to Damon freedom, others sneer
At Pythias' folly or feel pity for
His certain fate.
    Now from Ortygia come
An hundred hoplites of the royal guard,
And with them workmen, who at once begin,
With busy handicraft, to frame and raise
Within the Agora the lofty stage
Of death, whereon to all shall be displayed
The execution of the tyrant's will.

Around, an ever-growing multitude
Stands idly grouped to watch them at their task,
Whilst each from each fresh tidings seeks to gain.
Unto the greater part it is enough
To know that Pythias dies at set of sun,
And careless of aught else, they inly fret
And chide the slow revolving of the hours.
Fit subjects of despotic sway are these!
But clustered here and there, aloof from such,
Are patriots, who, in secret words, lament
A fallen state, and view, with heavy hearts,
The coming fate of one — whiche'er it be —
That perishes as Freedom's sacrifice.

The gnomon's changing shadow now hath marked
The noontide hour, and overhead the God
Of Day seems lingering in his course to learn
What mighty cause hath wrought such change below,
That, in the fields untilled, no husbandman
Appears, and on the lonely sea no gleam
Of sail, whilst all the homes and public ways
Of Syracuse are tenantless and still,
And through the city is no sign of life,
Save only there within the Agora,
Where countless thousands mingle in the host,
Restless and surging, yet forever held
And bound by that which fills the common gaze.
In this o'ercrowded mart hath Commerce e'er

Maintained her place, but now her voice is still.
And not, methinks, to-day, would such as bend
The knee to Plutus[1] seek their wonted gains.
The radiant god, whose high, imperial car
Stays not in its eternal path, begins
His downward course, and heedless whether life
Or death befall, draws nearer to his goal.
His slanting beams still light a steadfast sea
Of upturned faces, gazing now at him
To mete how soon, departing, he shall rest
Upon the western ridge; yet oftener there
Where ready waits the grim machine of death,
Protected by the guardsmen's circling steel;
While yonder, on Ortygia's crowded walls,
Are men-at-arms, in glittering panoply,
Who look amazed upon the mighty throng,
And wait the hour when, girded by their spears,
The tyrant goes to mark how Pythias dies.
For who, from Dionysius to the least
Among his following, dreams that ere again
Will Damon willingly come back to meet
His awful doom? Event so strange would be
A wonder fit to be inscribed in bronze,
And kept for a perpetual memory
Among the public archives of the State.

---

[1] Plutus (Πλοῦτος) was the god of riches. Jupiter deprived him of sight that he might not bestow wealth on the righteous alone.

And of the multitude around the block
Only that band of Brothers, hither led
By mingled love and grief for him condemned,
Feeling a tie that others cannot feel,
And knowing well what faith and Friendship are,
Can say, with hearts wherein no doubt may rest,
That Damon will return in timely speed,
Eager for death, that Pythias may go free.

But soon the time hath passed which Damon had
Foretold should see his coming. Lower sinks
The lamp of day, and longer shadows warn
That soon the western hills will hide its beams.

What cause of unforeseen delay hath kept
Our Brother? Surely some calamity
Of gravest import hath befallen him!
Yet must he quickly come or Pythias dies.
One hour alone remains ere set of sun.
But if he come not! That may never be,
Unless the hand of death shall stay his steps.
Erelong Ortygia's walls resound the clang
Of brazen trumpets, which proclaim to all
Without that now the sovereign will approach;
And through the open portal swiftly ride
Armed knights, who hasten to the Agora,
And, sundering the throng, shout unto them
To make a way for Dionysius.

Strong files of hoplites follow next; and then,
In ranks compact, march forth the royal guard,
With, lo! the tyrant in the midst of them.
Around the place of death the phalanx forms,
And thus protected, Dionysius waits
Till to his presence Pythias shall be brought.

As on him, standing there, the level beams
Of sunset fall, methinks it strange that he,
A beardless youth, one, almost yesterday,
Unknown to fame, should now, as sovereign,
Be master of our fortunes, of our lives,
And lord it over Syracuse, the first
And greatest city of Trinacria.
And so do many wonder while they gaze,
For unto him alone all eyes are turned,
And everywhere a breathless silence reigns.

As when the surface of some tranquil lake,
Set bright and gem-like 'mid surrounding hills,
Ripples beneath the flitting mountain breeze
That in a single murmur lives and dies,
So as our Brother Pythias stands revealed
In Dionysius' presence, quickly riseth
The sound of many tongues, — then all is hushed.

Freed from his chains, erect the captive stands.
His manly countenance no lurking fear

Dishonors, but the beaming eye, the lips
Compressed, show triumph and a heart firm fixed
In high and noble purpose.
     Unto him
The tyrant sternly saith, "The hour's at hand
Appointed for the death of Damon. There,
On yon horizon, sits the parting orb ;
Thus lingereth o'er its grave thy sun of life.
Thy friend hath not returned, so thou must die!"

"Tyrant, I welcome death! The prison-house
Hath heard my prayer that thus might come the end.
Ready and willing, I await the stroke
That gives me death, and Damon liberty!"

"But car'st thou nothing for the joyful light
Of life? Behold'st thou not around thee friends,
Who weep for thee, departing thus untimely?
Seest thou not how 'neath the day's last smile,
All Syracuse is robed in rays of splendor?
And art thou willing, leaving thus the bloom
Of life and dear companionship of friends,
To bear the gloomy silence of the tomb?"

"Mine eyes, indeed, behold the vision, yet
Beholding it they seem to tell my soul
More loudly of the happiness the friend
Best loved shall taste when I have passed away."

"But canst thou deem him friend that shamelessly
Betrayed thee into suffering the doom
Pronounced on him?   Recall the lying words
Whereby, within the dungeon-keep, he feigned
To give thee firm assurance that betimes
He would return to rescue thee from death.
Too well knew I the falseness of his heart!
But tell me, where, where now are those firm ties
Of Brotherhood that bound thee unto him?
Like ropes of sand are these in such an hour!"

"No, Dionysius.   Neither danger's form
Nor love of life can rend those sacred ties,
Or move the steadfast soul of him on whom
They rest.   Say not that Damon is withheld
By fear of aught thy power could e'er inflict!
He hath not come; the cause, — it matters not.
Enough for me if he doth live.   Perchance,
His friends detain him, or the tearful woe
Of wife and child his reason hath o'erwhelmed
Naught else, methinks, could have so long delayed
His coming, in fulfilment of his word."

"Fool that thou art!   He never will return!
Nor hath his purpose dreamed of turning back!
Far less would be my wonder should the sea
Now glow beneath another rising sun,
Or should yon fortress sink beneath the waves

That idly beat against its walls, than if
Thine eyes amazed should ever look again
Upon thy faithless friend in Syracuse.
Headsman, perform thy duty! Yet delay
But for an instant; still some golden beams
O'erpass the western ridge. But when the last
Departing ray hath left the gilded top
Of yonder gnomon, strike and kill this man!"

What midnight silence now unbroken reigns!
The mighty host, unmoving, speechless, look
Upon the common centre, where is seen,
Amidst a forest dense of glittering steel,
Our Brother kneeling at the fatal block,
The tyrant and the headsman standing nigh,
With others, who with eagerness await
The signal when shall fall the mortal stroke.
The Agora is an unbroken sea
Of thick-compacted human life, and far
Away, vast multitudes have densely thronged
The temples, house-tops, and whatever place
May yield a foothold for the venturous gaze.

In that dread moment did our little band
Of Brothers mourn that Pythias was to die?
Ay! even as our sorrow-laden hearts
Made moan for Damon; for right well we knew
That death alone had kept him from our sight.

A gesture from the tyrant, and swift mounts
The headsman's gleaming sword. Our eyes are turned
Away. One gride of steel, and all were o'er!
We tremble as we listen for the sound, —
We tremble, yet the death-blow cometh not.
But why? Oh, wonder! when the headsman raised
The deadly blade, his vision caught afar,
Upon the loftier heights, the forms of men
Whose frantic arms were waving unto him,
As if to stay his hand; and to his ears
Was borne the mingled chorus of their shouts,
High raised and loud and ever wilder shrilled.
He wavered 'twixt the doing and the deed;
And in that instant Dionysius saw
The far-off tumult, and the outcries heard,
And quickly turning, bade the headsman pause.

And well, indeed, may all men stand amazed,
For as of mighty tempest comes the roar
Of countless voices. Nearer now it swells,
And yonder, lo! the massy crowd hath surged
To right and left, and through the path there made
A horseman spurs his steed, and hitherward
Urgeth his headlong course. "Make way! make way!"
"Thank God! 'tis he, that in this latest hour
Hath come to save his friend!" Amidst a shout
That rifts the vault of heaven, swift as light

He fleets unto the block where Pythias kneels,
And leaping from his steed — that sinks and dies —
Enwraps that Brother in his arms, and weeps.

Pale, speechless, thunderstruck the tyrant stands,
Nor word nor motion tells his secret thought.

Now 'twixt ecstatic joy and lingering tears,
No more can Damon utter than, " Saved! saved!
My Pythias, thou are saved! " Then crieth he,
" Thou livest, best-loved Brother, and in thee,
The half of mine own soul, live I a life
Restored. What anguish and what dreadful fear
Have filled my breast! My thankful, joyful heart
Beats wildly as I see thee safe, and haste
To meet my doom. Yet ere I 'm cold in death,
Hear thou my tale, and hearing it, forgive!
Released by thee, I hastened to my home
And quickly bade farewell to wife and child.
Then, early, timely, I set forth on my
Return. I know not what of fear for thee
Oppressed me. Onward flew my foaming steed,
In furious haste, — he fell, and there he died.
Dashed to the earth, I lay as one deprived
Of life, and when at length I oped mine eyes,
The orb of day had sunk far toward its bourne,
And thou and Syracuse were far away!
A madness seized me! Loudly then I called

On heaven and earth to save thee from thy fate, —
To help me on my way! In vain, in vain!
Only the hideous echoes mocked my voice.
But whilst I stood bereft of reason; lo!
A horseman swiftly passed me on the road.
I shouted unto him; he stayed his course,
He listened to my words, and to that man,
Lucullus, the Italian, — for I learned
His name and nation, — owest thou thy life,
And I, that now I may depart in peace.
In me, by proof that never errs, he found
A Brother. From his steed he quickly sprang.
Then helping me to mount, bade me God speed:
And so I hastened unto Syracuse.
Now, headsman, I am ready. I await
The blow. Farewell, my Brother!"

          Then aloud
Cries Pythias, "Stay! 'tis I, 'tis I that wait
The blow! Thou shalt not die, my Brother! I
Alone am now reserved for death."
            "This hour
Of dread hath crazed thee, Pythias! Loose from me
Thy grasp. 'Tis I who am condemned to die."

"Ay! but too late thou cam'st, the time was past.
To Dionysius I appeal! Stand back!

Unhand me! Let me kneel again beside
The block!"
    "What madness, Pythias, fills thy soul?
I have thee now secure. Thou shalt not move.
To Dionysius I too will appeal,
Knowing full well what judgment he will pass."

So unto Dionysius all men turn.
Yet pale, unmoving, speechless, long he stands;
Then sudden waking, as one from a dream,
He straight commands, "Let silence be proclaimed!"

The gloom of eventide is closing in;
But on the western hills a purple mound
Of fading light is piled as o'er a grave.
Now like a requiem for departed day
A mingled strain of trumpets riseth, wild
And mournful on the air, and sinks and dies.
Then all is still.
    High raised above the vast
And silent throng, intent upon his words,
Stands Dionysius. For a moment, as
In thought, he opens not his mouth; and then
He calmly speaks, that those afar may hear: —

"Mark ye my words, O men of Syracuse,
Learn what your sovereign's will and pleasure is.

"Beside me are two Brothers, bound by ties
Of Fellowship, to me a mystery.
Of these two Brothers, Damon, for offence
Against my royal majesty, was doomed
To die.
  "That ere the appointed hour
He might behold his home and bid his wife
And child farewell, his Brother, Pythias, took
Upon himself to wear his chains, and meet
For him his doom, should he return no more.
Then Damon was released and went to seek
His home. And now, from home and wife and child
And liberty, he swiftly hastens back
To rescue Pythias' life and yield his own.
When Pythias took upon himself these chains,
E'en for an instant could the dread of death
O'ercome the generous purpose of his love?
When Damon felt again the joys of home,
The happiness of freedom, could his soul
Forget the peril of his captive friend?
Judge ye, who have beheld this wondrous scene,
And tell me, for I know not, which hath best
Observed the tie of Friendship.
    "Each of them
Now begs for death, that so his friend may live.

"But hearken unto my imperial will!
To Pythias I give back the liberty

That unto him most rightfully belongs;
And unto Damon just release I grant,
And now and here my pardon I extend.
Long years of peace and happiness abide
With both! And if this wish avail, may I
Be made a third in their firm Fellowship!"

He ended; and from all the dusky gloom
Thousands on thousands joined in wild acclaim,
And gave, with one accord, a mighty shout,
That startled Night upon her ebon throne;
And broad Trinacria trembled with the sound;
And far away the waves of ocean leaped.

He ended; and the hours of night began,
But night so full of joy as that, I ween,
Was never known before in Syracuse.

APPENDIX

To the Story of Damon and Pythias.

A.

Ætna. — Ætna (in Italian, *Monte Gibello*, or, by contraction, *Mongibello*), situated on the east coast of Sicily, in the province of Catania (formerly Catana), is one of the highest mountains in Europe, rising to an altitude of nearly 11,000 feet from the level of the sea. Although composed, properly speaking, of many large mountains, its formation presents the general appearance of an immense obtuse cone, standing isolated and distinct, and terminated superiorly by the smoking mouth of the crater.

A second principal crater, produced by the dreadful eruption of 1669, exists near its summit, and many smaller ones are to be seen on its sides, but all of these are extinct.

Ætna is divided into three zones, of which the lowest is very fertile and populous, containing a population of about 300,000; the second is a wooded region, covered with forests of oak, pine, and chestnut trees: one of the last variety is large enough to afford shelter to one hundred horsemen, whence the Italian call it *cento cavalli;* finally, rises a desert region, at the summit of which is the crater, more than three miles in circumference, and always in activity. This part of the mountain Pindar called "the nurse of keen snow all the year long," and the contrast of its fires and snows is dwelt on by later writers. From this region Sicily is supplied with ice. The circumference of Ætna at its base is not less than one hundred miles, and some writers have nearly doubled this estimate. From its top the view extends, in clear weather, from Vesuvius to the island of Malta. Ætna is celebrated in fable, for under it Jupiter had chained an offending giant, variously said to have been Typhon, Enceladus, and Briareus.

In the following lines Virgil describes this burning mountain, and recounts the myth which served to explain its eruptions: —

> " Portus ab accessu ventorum immotus, et ingens
> Ipse; sed horrificis juxtà tonat Ætna ruinis,
> Interdumque atram prorumpit ad æthera nubem,
> Turbine fumantem piceo et candente favillâ;
> Attollitque globos flammarum, et sidera lambit:
> Interdum scopulos avulsaque viscera montis
> Erigit eructans, liquefactaque saxa sub auras
> Cum gemitu glomerat, fundoque exaestuat imo.
> Fama est, Enceladi semiustum fulmine corpus
> Urgueri mole hâc, ingentemque insuper Ætnam
> Impositam ruptis flammam exspirare caminis;
> Et fessum quotiens mutet latus, intremere omnem
> Murmure Trinacriam, et coelum subtexere fumo."
> *Æn.*, III, 570-582.

> " The port, capacious and secure from wind,
> Is to the foot of thund'ring Ætna joined.
> By turns a pitchy cloud she rolls on high,
> By turns hot embers from her entrails fly,
> And flakes of mountain flames, that lick the sky.
> Oft from her bowels massy rocks are thrown,
> And, shiver'd by the force, come piecemeal down.
> Oft liquid lakes of burning sulphur flow,
> Fed from the fiery springs that boil below.
> Enceladus, they say, transfix'd by Jove,
> With blasted limbs came tumbling from above;

And, where he fell, th' avenging father drew
This flaming hill, and on his body threw.
As often as he turns his weary sides,
He shakes the solid isle, and smoke the heavens hides."
Dryden's Translation.

Mythology also placed in the caverns of Ætna the smithy of the Cyclopes, a savage race of one-eyed giants, who there assisted Vulcan in forging the thunderbolts of Jupiter and the arms of the gods and celebrated heroes.

The first known eruption took place in the time of Pythagoras, and of this Pindar, who called the mountain "the pillar of heaven" (κίων οὐρανοῦ) makes mention. In the reign of Dionysius the Elder, two eruptions occurred. During one of these, Plato, who was then a guest at the tyrant's court, was invited by the Catanians to visit them and study the phenomena of their famous volcano.

The lava of Ætna ingulfed the ancient cities of Naxos, Hybla, and Inessa. The eruption of 1183 destroyed Catania with 15,000 persons; in that of 1669, which lasted several months, 20,000 lives were lost; in that of 1693, sixty villages were consumed, and 18,000 of their inhabitants perished. The last eruption took place in 1865.

B.

SYRACUSE. — Founded B. C. 735 by a colony of Corinthians under Archias, Syracuse soon became the most important city in Sicily. Its population at the time of its capture by the Romans was about 1,000,000. Its early form of government was republican. Ruled afterwards by kings, Gelon (484–478), Hiero (478–467), and Thrasybulus (467–466), it recovered its independence and was (466–

405) governed as a democracy. It was in the last interval, 414, that the attack of Athens was victoriously repulsed and the long struggle with Carthage began. Dionysius the Elder became tyrant B. C. 405 and reigned until 367. After him ruled Dionysius the Younger (367-357), Dion (357-354), Callipe (354-353), Hipparinus (353-351), Nypsius (351-347), and Dionysius the Younger, restored from exile (347-343). Timoleon (343) re-established the republic; Sosostratus (320-317) destroyed it. But it was again re-established by Agathocles (317-289) and survived after his death for twenty years. The Romans took the city, B. C. 212, after a three years' siege, in spite of the wonders accomplished by the genius of Archimedes in its defence.

In one of his orations against Verres, Cicero gives a detailed description of Syracuse, which has been elegantly translated by Dr. Smith as follows:—

"You have often heard that Syracuse was the largest of all Greek cities and most beautiful of all cities. And it is both, indeed. For it is strong by its natural position, and striking to behold from whatever side it is approached, whether by land or sea. It has two ports, as it were, enclosed within the buildings of the city itself, so as to combine with it from every point of view, which have different and separate entrances, but are united and conjoined together at the opposite extremity. The junction of these separates from the mainland the part of the town called the Island [Ortygia], but this is reunited to the continent by a bridge across the narrow strait which divides them. So great is the city that it may be said to consist of four cities, all of them of large size; one of which is that which I have already mentioned, the Island, which is surrounded by the two ports, while it projects towards the mouth and entrance of each of them. In it is the palace of King Hiero, which is now the customary residence of our pretors. It contains also several sacred edifices, but two in particular which far surpass the others; one, a temple of Diana, the other, of Minerva [Athena], which before the arrival of Verres was most highly adorned. At the extremity of this island is a fountain of fresh water, which has the name of Arethusa, of incredible magnitude and full of fish This would be wholly overflowed and covered by the waves were it not separated from the sea by a strongly built barrier of stone. The second city of Syracuse is that which is called Achradina, which contains a forum [Agora] of very large size, beautiful porticos, a most highly ornamented Prytaneum, a spacious Curia, and a magnificent temple of Jupiter Olympus; not to speak of the other parts of the city, which are occupied by private buildings, being divided by one broad street through its whole length and many cross streets. The third city is that which is called Tycha, because it contains a very ancient temple of Fortune. In this is a very spacious gymnasium as well as many sacred edifices. The fourth city is that which because it was last built was called Neapolis, at the top of which is a theatre of vast size; besides it contains two splendid temples, one of Ceres, the other of Libera, and a statue of Apollo, which is known by the name of Temenites, of great beauty and very large size, which Verres would not have hesitated to carry off if he had been able to remove it." — *Cic.*, *Verr.*, IV, 52, 53.

This description, although written at a later period, very nearly represents the more important features of the older parts of the town in the time of Dionysius. The citadel of Syracuse, which was rebuilt by Dionysius the Elder, probably stood in that part of Ortygia which faced Achradina, and if so, looked directly upon the Agora or marketplace. Achradina extended inland and about three miles along the sea-coast. That part of it which was close to Ortygia consisted of low ground level with the island, but the remaining and larger part lay on a range of heights which stretched for several miles inland and were divided from the low land by a natural wall of rock. After Dionysius became tyrant, he removed the causeway, of which Cicero speaks, and by constructing additional fortifications and docks, converted Ortygia into an impregnable fortress.

The Latomiæ or Lithotomiæ were originally quarries excavated in the rocks that divided the upper from the lower part of Achradina, whence the stone for the construction of the city was drawn. They are from sixty to eighty feet deep. Soon after being opened they served as prisons, and on the surrender of Nicias, the whole (7,000) of the Athenian prisoners were confined in them, and most of them died. One of them, of large size, situated near the remains of an ancient theatre, is planted with a great variety of fruit trees. On one side of it, cut into the rock, is the remarkable excavation which, from its fancied resemblance to the human tympanum, has been called "The Ear of Dionysius." "It is in the shape of a parabolic curve, ending in an elliptical arch, with sides parallel to its axis, perfectly smooth, and covered with a slight stalactitic incrustation that renders its repercussions amazingly sonorous. It has an awful and gloomy appearance, which, with its singular shape, perhaps gave rise to the popular and amusing paradox that Dionysius had it constructed for the confinement of those whom he deemed inimical to his authority, and that from the little apartment above it he could overhear all the conversation among the prisoners."
—*Capt. Smith's Memoir, descriptive of Sicily.*

C.

ACRAGAS. — This city was situated on the south coast of Sicily, a little to the southeast of modern Girgenti, between the rivers Hypsas (*fiume Drago*) and Acragas (*fiume di san Biagio*). It was founded in B. C. 582 by a Dorian colony from Gela, and became very flourishing in commerce and agriculture. The capture of the city by the Carthaginians, here referred to, took place in the latter part of December, B. C. 406, after a siege of eight months. In B. C. 210 it came under the dominion of the Romans, by whom it was known as Agrigentum.

Acragas was built upon several hills, on the highest of which was the citadel. At the time of the Carthaginian siege it contained about 300,000 inhabitants. The estimate of Diogenes Laërtius, that its population amounted to 800,000, is clearly excessive.

Virgil mentions this place, together with several others referred to in this poem, in his description of the voyage of Æneas from Ortygia to Cape Pachynus, and thence along the south coast of Sicily: —

> " Sicanio praetenta sinu jacet insula contra
> Plemmyrium undosum: nomen dixere priores
> Ortygiam. Alpheum fama est huc Elidis amnem
> Occultas egisse vias subter mare; qui nunc
> Ore, Arethusa, tuo Siculis confunditur undis.
> Jussi numina magna loci veneramur; et inde
> Exsupero praepingue solum stagnantis Helori.
> Hinc altas cautes projectaque saxa Pachyni
> Radimus, et fatis numquam concessa moveri
> Adparet Camarina procul campique Geloi,
> Immanisque Gela fluvii cognomine dicta.
> Arduus inde Acragas ostentat maxima longe
> Moenia, **magnanimum** quondam generator equorum;

Teque datis linquo ventis, palmosa Selinus,
Et vada dura lego saxis Lilybeïa caecis."
Æn., III, 692-707.

Outstretched before Sicania's bay, against
Plemmyrium's billowy strand, an island lies;
Its name the forefathers Ortygia called.
Hither, they say, Alpheus, Elis' stream,
Forced hidden channels 'neath the sea; and now
By thy fount, Arethusa, is it blent
With the Sicilian waves. As bidden, we
The mighty local deities adore;
And thence I pass the soil exceeding rich
Of stagnating Helorus. Then we skirt
Pachynus' lofty "crags that warning give,"
And jutting rocks; and never by the Fates
Allowed to be removed, far, far away,
Appeareth Camarina to our view,
Geloan plains and Gela's monstrous town,
That from the river takes its name. And then
High Acragas its walls immense displays,
Once the producer of high-mettled steeds;
And thee, palm-clad Selinus, next I leave,
With favoring winds, and coast along the shoals
Of Lilybeum, rough with hidden reefs.

D.

DIONYSIUS. — Dionysius the Elder was born at Syracuse B C. 430. Of his early life very little is known, except that for a time he filled the position of scrivener or clerk in one of the public offices, and was afterwards a common soldier in the Syracusan army. He also joined the partisans of Hermocrates, and was severely wounded while engaged with them in an unsuccessful attempt to overthrow the democratic government of his native city. But up to the time of his remarkable speech in the *ecclesia*, he seems to have taken no prominent part in public affairs.

As to the effect of his violent exhortation on that occasion we have only such information as is contained in the narratives of Plato and Diodorus, and these are in hopeless conflict. The author has accordingly been compelled to meet the difficulty thereby presented as best he could. The account of Plato would seem to be of higher authority, because he was both a contemporary of Dionysius and for some time a guest at his court; while the Historical Library of Diodorus was written between three and four centuries after the event. Upon this doubtful point Mr. Grote appends a learned and exhaustive note in Vol. X of his "History of Greece." The general conclusion, however, at which that eminent historian arrives is open to many objections. In describing the various steps whereby Dionysius rose to absolute power, occupying in all a period of not more than five or six months, the poem conforms substantially to the narrative of Diodorus.

Dionysius was twenty-five years of age when he began to reign. His proscriptions and injustice raised against him many conspiracies and two revolts, which he suppressed. All his reign was occupied, 1st, In strengthening himself in Syracuse; 2d, In driving the Carthaginians out of Sicily, and extending his dominion over the entire island; 3d, In conquering the Greek towns in the south of Italy. In the first war against the Carthaginians, while he held the position of general autocrator, he had yielded to them Gela and Camarina; but in 403 he captured Enna, Catana, Naxos, Leontini, and Messené. Defeated by Himilco in 396, and besieged by him in Syracuse, he nevertheless took Taurimenium at the close of the war. From

394 to 384 Italy occupied his attention. He made himself master of Locris in 389, and of Crotona, after a hard resistance, in 387. He formed an alliance with the Gauls, the conquerors of Rome, in 390, and also founded some colonies on the west coast of the Adriatic, and ravaged Etruria. After a third undecisive war with the Carthaginians, he captured. in 368, Selinus, Entella, and Eryx. Death alone prevented him from driving the Carthaginians out of Sicily.

Cicero represents him as a tyrant in the worst sense. It is certain, however, that he restored independence to Sicily, enriched and enlarged Syracuse, increased her arsenals, fortifications, and marine, and fostered letters and the arts. He is said to have cultivated poetry and history, medicine and surgery. His horses raced at the Olympic games, where his chariots were broken and his poems hissed. And even in his own court Philoxenus, a poet of Cythera, found fault with his verses, and for this offence was committed to Lithotomiæ. But Athens at last crowned one of his tragedies, and Dionysius, to celebrate the event, gave a grand banquet, at which he ate and drank so intemperately that he fell senseless and soon after died. According to others, he was poisoned by his son. His death took place in 367, and he had, accordingly, reigned thirty-eight years.

Dionysius was married twice. His first wife perished in the *émeute* which followed the return of the knights from Gela to Syracuse. Afterward he married two wives at the same time, and each of them, it is said, continued to hold an equal share in his affection. By one of these he had two sons and two daughters, and by the other, Dionysius the Younger, who succeeded him.

E.

PYTHAGORAS. — This illustrious philosopher was born at Samos, about B. C. 569. At Lesbos he was a pupil of Pherecydes, and at Miletus of Thales and Anaximander. He was also instructed by Hermodamas at Samos, and having been advised by him to complete his education by extensive travel, visited Phœnicia and subsequently went to reside in Egypt, which was then regarded by the Greeks as the repository of the highest wisdom. Here he acquired from the priests of Isis and Osiris a knowledge of their theocratic and sacerdotal systems, together with the elements of numbers and geometry and the language of symbols and hieroglyphics. Here, too, he was taught the doctrine of metempsychosis, but whether he accepted and applied this belief in its literal sense is somewhat doubtful. After he had lived in Egypt twenty-two years (547-525), that country was conquered by the armies of Cambyses, and according to Jamblichus, Pythagoras was led in captivity to Babylon, where he remained twelve years. During this interval, he acquired from the Chaldæans and Magi the principles of astronomy, astrology, and medicine, and also gained a knowledge of the religions of India and was initiated into the doctrines of Zoroaster. On his return to Greece, 512, having visited Sparta, Elis, and Delphi, he attempted to found a school of philosophy in his native Samos, but was prevented by the hostility of Polycrates, who was then tyrant of the island.

He then left Samos and went, preceded by an illustrious reputation, to Crotona in Southern Italy. Here he taught and established a secret society which was composed of the richest and noblest citizens. For a long time this association was very prosperous, but it was finally broken up by a popular insurrection, in which most of its members perished. Pythagoras subsequently retired to Metapontum, where he died at a very advanced age.

Pythagoras himself, although perhaps the most learned philosopher of antiquity, wrote nothing. A collection of his maxims, called The Golden Verses, was probably written by his pupil, Lycis.

To Pythagoras is due in mathematics the discovery of various properties of numbers, the demonstration of the value of the hypothenuse, and of some other geometric theorems; in physics, the mathematical theory of musical sounds; in astronomy, certain elementary notions regarding the movements of the sun, moon, and planets, which, though falling far short of the theory of Copernicus, were greatly in advance of the previous cosmographic ideas of the Greeks. In the centre of the universe he placed the "central-fire," which his disciple Philolaus termed "the hearth of the universe, the watch-tower of Zeus." Around this the heavenly bodies revolved; farthest off, the fixed stars, then, in order, the planets, the sun, moon, earth, and "counter-earth" (ἀντίχθων), the last being "a sort of other half of the earth, a distinct body from it, but always moving equal to it." The heavenly bodies were divided by certain intervals corresponding to those of the musical scale, and by its motion, each of them produced a certain note, determined by the distance of the body from the "central-fire." Hence arose the celebrated doctrine of "the music of the spheres." According to Cicero, Pythagoras held that God was the soul of the world diffused through all its parts. As all numbers are evolved from unity, so he claimed that from the primary unit or monad (God) all the universe was evolved. The Supreme Being had first created the "immortal gods," then *heroes* (or *angels*, as some commentators understand), and last of all, as being least in dignity, man. He also recognized in God the moral governor of a moral universe. Souls that had lived ill, remained, after their earth-life, in the gulf of Hecate until purged of their impurities; the souls of the just went to an abode of happiness above the moon.

Long after the death of Pythagoras, many fraternities bearing his name and modelled after his plan continued to exist; but all of them were at last consolidated with similar associations, called Orphic societies, in Greece. It is likely that the severe rules of discipline which he had imposed on his followers became relaxed after his decease, and that Fraternity was recognized to be the chief, as it always had been a principal, bond of their union.

From the accounts which various authors give of the Pythagorean societies or brotherhoods, it appears: 1. There were degrees or gradations among the members themselves. 2. The members were devotedly attached to each other and were willing to sacrifice fortune or peril life in each other's behalf. (This is attested by Porphyrius and Jamblichus.) 3. Whatever was taught or done among the members was kept a profound secret. 4. They had secret conventional symbols by which members who had never met before could recognize each other. (*Schol. ad Arist. Nub.*, 611; *Jamb*, 237, 238; *Krische*, pp. 43, 44.) That the principles which were taught among them were correct is evident from the fact that the various Pythagoreans mentioned in history are all represented to have been good and honorable men.

www.ingramcontent.com/pod-product-compliance
Lightning Source LLC
Chambersburg PA
CBHW020057170426
43199CB00009B/309